KITCHEN GARDENS
IN CONTAINERS

KITCHEN GARDENS
IN CONTAINERS

Antony Atha

Sterling Publishing Company, Inc. New York

First paperback edition published in 2002
by Sterling Publishing Co.,
387 Park Avenue South, New York,
NY 10016, USA

First published in Great Britain in 2000
by Collins & Brown Limited

Distributed in Canada by Sterling
Publishing c/o Canadian Manda Group,
One Atlantic Avenue, Suite 105, Toronto,
Ontario, Canada M6K 3E7

Library of Congress Cataloging-in-
Publication Data Available

9 8 7 6 5 4 3 2 1

Sterling ISBN 0-8069-9293-X (PB)

Project editor Ulla Weinberg
Edited and designed by axis design
Picture researcher Liz Moore

Reproduction by Hong Kong Graphic &
Printing Ltd

Printed and bound by Paramount Printing
Co. Ltd, Hong Kong

Contents

Foreword

A container kitchen garden must fulfil three purposes. Most importantly it must provide the gardener with a sense of satisfaction – gardeners growing their own herbs, fruit and vegetables in containers must feel that they have achieved something worthwhile. Secondly, the garden must provide the cook with fresh produce that is both nutritious and provides a talking point at the dinner table. And finally, the design of any container garden must be attractive, it must be a pleasant place to sit in and look at. It should contain a variety of containers as well as plants, and if possible the containers should be placed at different levels to allow the eye to travel up and down.

THE IMPORTANCE OF PLANNING

Any container garden needs to be planned extremely carefully. By their nature they are restricted for space and they therefore need more planning and more thought than a large traditional garden where space between border, vegetable patches and lawns can be adjusted and color added with flowers and flowering shrubs. The most important thing for all container kitchen gardens is the exposure. It is vital to take into account the direction the garden faces for this is the one thing that you cannot alter. Many, many plants will only thrive if they can be grown in the sun or conversely,

CENTER *Low-growing herbs are excellent plants for shallow containers and permanent displays can be given interest by evergreen box topiary.*

LEFT *Small lemon trees have a dual purpose for they add color and scent outside in summer and make good house plants in winter.*

the shade. There are lists of plants and charts showing which plants will grow in which position on pages 154–5 of this book.

SIZE AND PURPOSE

The gardener also has to decide how ambitious the garden is to be. If the garden is large enough to accommodate some large raised beds and permanent containers, then fruit trees and climbers can be planted to provide blossom and fruit in spring and summer. The traditional use for a container garden is to grow herbs. Most herbs grow well in containers, particularly the more vigorous varieties such as mint and rosemary, as their roots can be contained. The cook must only step outside the kitchen door to cut fresh herbs each day, and with imagination a herb garden can be interesting, useful and attractive.

designing
Container
gardens

All successful gardens fulfil a purpose. They please the eye and provide a blend of color and shape to enhance the beauty of the house they surround. This is as true for a container garden as it is for any garden with a large formal design. Container gardens are usually planned and planted on a small scale and great care has to be taken with each component so that the perfect blend is achieved. This is particularly so for the edible container garden, for as well as providing herbs, fruit and vegetables for the kitchen, it must be designed and planted so that it embellishes the patio or balcony on which it is placed.

LEFT *Color, texture and form all contribute to the impact of the finished garden. Here, vivid lavender wooden benches and muted terracotta tiles frame a trailing arrangement of eggplants and flat-leaf parsley in a glazed earthenware container.*

Using the Available Space

Even the smallest patio garden should not reveal its secrets all at once. Plan the positioning of the containers so that you have to walk in curves and around corners to find out what comes next.

ABOVE RIGHT An attractive strawberry planter is a must in all container gardens for it contributes color, flowers and fruit.

The first thing any gardener has to do when planning a garden is to measure the available space. This is particularly important when planning a kitchen container garden for when space is limited greater care has to be taken to make sure every bit is used to the best advantage.

RIGHT *Even the smallest garden can include a focal point to catch the eye. A decorative terracotta pot with an old-fashioned lavender is most effective.*

Whether the space is large or small two fundamental rules apply: all the elements of the garden must be easily reachable, and there must be a clear plan to the area. These may seem elementary, even unnecessary, but planning involves simple things, such as allowing space to walk out of the back door, making sure you can reach all the containers to water them, allowing access to an outside tap, and checking the position of any windows so that growing plants will not obstruct the light. It is surprising how often such practicalities are forgotten.

If your container garden is a window box or on a small balcony then there is usually little choice about how the space can be organized and used.

If the container garden is on a patio or roof garden then you have to think about all the likely uses for the space. Is it used for eating out in the summer or sunbathing? Is it an extra room? Do the family sit there? How much competition for the space is there between the gardening and non-gardening members of the family?

RAISED BEDS AND POTAGERS

Once these questions have been answered you can decide, for instance, whether there is room for a raised bed around a patio area or whether the patio is large enough to create a miniature potager kitchen garden with small formal beds of herbs and vegetables.

Raised beds have a number of advantages: they are more easily reached by the elderly and disabled; they provide a garden with the large containers that are necessary if permanent trees and shrubs are to be grown; and they give a container garden more substance. If you plan to build one remember to allow space between the container and the walls of the house otherwise the siding would be damaged. Similarly, if you want to construct a potager take care not to interfere with the water or utility lines to the house or apartment.

THE VERTICAL DIMENSION

Height and different levels are another important consideration. Are you surrounded by a wall or trellis? Can you position containers so that you can grow climbing plants that will screen you from view? Is there sufficient wall space to grow trees and shrubs? Have you got walls that will support wall pots? Is it possible to plan arches or pergolas to cover a seating area with vines or other climbing plants? Two essential points in all garden design are access and surprise. No garden should give up its secrets at once. Try and achieve a dynamic practical flow, that carries you around the area, however small.

BELOW Containers of vegetables and herbs grouped in wicker baskets give differing levels and colors. This is a well thought-out design.

Aims and Objectives

Even small gardens must have form and color. Organize the containers into a pleasing, coherent pattern and grow plants with different shades of leaf color throughout the year.

ABOVE RIGHT *An alpine strawberry in fruit makes a decorative feature in a terracotta pot.*

BELOW *Purple eggplants are just one of the exotic vegetables that can be grown on a hot patio, trained up a cane.*

When you have finished planning out the space, you can start to implement the design. Draw the garden to scale on a piece of graph paper, putting in all the essential features, such as doors, windows, walls, fences and taps. Then transfer this design on to the ground marking out the areas you have chosen for containers in chalk on the patio or cut out sheets of paper to match the shapes of the containers. See whether this makes sense. Walk around them and change their position until you are completely satisfied. It is always possible to move containers but it is annoying to realize that a permanent feature such as a raised bed is not in the right place when you have spent money and effort building it.

EXPOSURE

This is an important consideration for any patio gardener and it is the one thing that cannot be changed. Check which direction your garden faces and assess how much sun it gets each day.

There is absolutely no point whatsoever trying to grow herbs from the Mediterranean, that by their very nature like heat and sun, if all you can offer them is a shady, north-facing patio. This is the basic rule for all gardens, disheartening or not. If you read the conditions that each plant prefers before planning, buying and planting, you will avoid considerable disappointment and also save money.

Decide what you hope to achieve. Annual herbs and vegetables can be varied from year to year but if you want to grow fruit trees you will probably need a south- or south-west-facing wall. Is there sufficient wall space? Fruit trees are relatively expensive, they require care and attention and this must be balanced against the pleasures of spring blossom and fresh fruit in the fall.

Do you want fresh herbs available for the cook throughout much of the year or do you want to grow a selection of special vegetables for special occasions? There are gardeners who will grow one Brussels sprout plant each year just so that they can have the pleasure of eating their own sprouts at Christmas dinner. Everyone has their own priorities and you may have to compromise.

COLOR AND FORM

Whatever your priorities it is important to think of the balance of color and form in a container garden. Containers of vegetables and herbs should please the eye as well as the palate. Plan to have a selection of leaf colors; try and grow two or three red cabbages that can stand in the container until well into the fall; break up the shape by growing dwarf trees in tubs, adding height and form to the garden; vary the levels of the containers, and make sure that the herb containers include attractive gold, purple-leaved and variegated varieties. Try to imagine the different greens of the various vegetables and plant them so they will contrast with each another.

Finally position a strawberry planter so that the white flowers can be seen from the windows in late spring, and the bright red fruits in summer.

BELOW *Even a fairly small tub can contain a large bay tree that can be clipped into shape. Provide support if the tree is in an exposed position.*

Designing with Herb Containers

The secret of successful design in gardening lies in care, planning and study. Think carefully about the objectives and possibilities, and don't be afraid to experiment to get the effect you want.

ABOVE RIGHT Keeping herbs in containers means they can easily be moved to the best situation as weather conditions change throughout the year.

BELOW The contrasting leaf shapes and colors of popular garden herbs – parsley, sage, chives and thyme – are combined here to good effect, while invasive mint is confined to its own container.

Many gardeners use containers to grow herbs, whatever the size of their garden. This has many advantages: the containers can be positioned just outside the kitchen door so that they are easily available to the cook; many herbs, such as mint, are invasive in the ground and are better confined to a pot; and a number of herbs are tender and are best brought indoors in winter or, if that is not possible, sheltered by the walls of the house or covered with protective mulch.

However, to expand your horizons beyond a few pots of culinary herbs and devote a whole patio to growing herbs while creating an attractive garden at the same time, requires more care and study. The secret of successful design in all gardening lies in these things; design is not some esoteric talent given to a few.

TELLING A STORY

Look at the space and how you plan to use it. Does the design work? It's no good lining up ranks of containers to fill a patio if you can't reach the troughs furthest away from you to prune a climbing rose or weed the plants.

If you are planning to devote a whole area to herbs, it's necessary to have a coherent planting plan. Try and get the containers to tell a story or concentrate on different aspects of herb gardening – scented, medicinal, culinary – or herbs from different parts of the world.

RIGHT At its simplest, a container herb garden may consist of just a few favorite culinary herbs, kept in pots on the kitchen windowsill for easy harvesting.

Designing with Herb Containers

RIGHT Low bowls will support annual herbs, such as these nasturtiums, that can be trained into elegant shapes.

THE BASICS OF COLOR AND FORM

A garden devoted solely to container herbs has to be planned meticulously to achieve the best possible contrast in color and form. Choose herbs with differently colored leaves, and vary the contents in each container; include scented herbs and medicinal plants. The design must please the eye and provide a contrast in colors and shape. This means two things: first a study of every plant to see whether they will go together, and second, a resolve to be ruthless with any mistakes you make. Everyone makes mistakes and all gardeners should be prepared to dig up plants, move them around or, if necessary, throw them away. A container garden has little space and it is most important to use this to the best possible advantage.

ROSES FOR A WALL

One of the first rules in planting is tallest at the back, shortest at the front. Start with a wall or trellis and decide how you are going to tackle it. There are not that

RIGHT Matching pots of lavender echo the lavender hedge of a formal garden. Here the containers have been raised and the hedge appears at eye level so the beautiful scent is more immediate. Trailing ivy hides the edges.

many herbal climbers available and possibly the best would be an old-fashioned climbing rose, such as *R. bracteata*, the 'Macartney Rose' from China (it needs a warm wall), *R.* 'Blairii Number Two', an old Bourbon rose, 'Climbing Ophelia', the climbing version of the old hybrid tea rose or *R. moschata*, an old musk rose probably introduced in the time of Queen Elizabeth I. All these roses are deliciously scented and the flowers can be used in the kitchen or dried for pot pourris.

OTHER CLIMBING PLANTS

Alternative climbing plants might include common jasmine (*Jasminum officinale*) with its fragrant small white flowers or the golden hop (*Humulus lupulus* 'Aureus'), although both are vigorous plants that may need to be confined.

GOOD BEDFELLOWS

Varieties of the common sage (*Salvia officinalis*) can be grown in one container to paint an abstract picture of varied leaf colors: common sage has gray-green woolly leaves; 'Icterina' has variegated yellow and green leaves; 'Kew Gold', golden-yellow leaves with touches of green; Purpurascens Group, red-purple young leaves that turn gray-green as they age; 'Tricolor', gray-green leaves edged with cream, pink and purple. A bonus is that salvias may be evergreen given a sheltered position in winter.

PLAN A VARIETY OF CONTAINERS

Decide how many containers you are going to plant and lay them all out in position until the groupings seem right. You could devote one container to medicinal herbs and research old herbals to learn exactly how each plant was used in medieval times.

A container of flowering medicinal plants looks lovely in the summer and could include calamint (*Calamintha* spp.), Californian poppies (*Eschscholzia* spp.), arnica (*Arnica* spp.), cornflowers (*Centaurea* spp.), with sweet woodruff (*Galium* spp.) as a ground-cover plant – or clumps of pink thrift (*Armeria* spp.).

ABOVE *Thymus vulgaris* 'Silver Posie' is one of the most popular varieties of common thyme with its lovely pale purple flowers that emerge in summer.

Designing with Herb Containers

SCENTED HERBS

Consider the scent of the plants as well as their other properties. Many herbs are beautifully scented and a container or two of scented herbs will perfume the air on a summer evening, something that is most welcome if the family is sitting outside. Scented herbs include heliotrope (*Heliotropium* spp.), sweet rocket (*Hesperis* spp.), hyssop (*Hyssopus* spp.), bergamot (*Monarda* spp.) with its scarlet flowers, sweet cicely (*Myrrhis* spp.), and the scented geranium (*Pelargonium* spp.) with sweet violets (*Viola odorata*) that can be planted at the front of the container to flower in spring.

KITCHEN HERBS

Containers of kitchen herbs can include a number of varieties of just one herb, such as mint, or herbs that appreciate the same growing conditions. Choose the varieties carefully to ensure that each container has different leaf colors and shapes to add interest. If the containers are devoted to herbs for the kitchen there are a number of possibilities. Several varieties of one herb in one container can look

RIGHT Basil, thyme, oregano and sage are among the herbs grouped in this terracotta pot. Color comes from purple-leaved basil. With care and planning a number of herbs can be grown together in a small space.

RIGHT A sunroom is a useful addition for the container kitchen gardener. Plants such as scented geraniums, lemon verbena and basil can be brought inside during the winter months.

18

very attractive: a pot of mint, for example, could include apple mint, spearmint, the larger peppermint at the back, eau de cologne or lemon mint, and Bowles's mint – the best for new potatoes – these would provide a contrast in color and form. Another idea would be to grow herbs from one part of the world, such as the Mediterranean. This is particularly suitable if you have a sunny open patio and can grow herbs that love the heat, such as thyme (*Thymus* spp.), oregano (*Origanum* spp.), sage (*Salvia* spp.) and rosemary (*Rosmarinus* spp.) – these herbs can all be grouped in a large container. Sages in particular come in many varieties and have leaves in contrasting colors of green and purple.

Herbs for Contrast

Use some containers for plants with gray leaves, such as lavender (*Lavandula* spp.) or the curry plant (*Helichrysum* spp.). These will look particularly effective if you position them against a dark background. Remember that colors have much more effect when grouped together. Also take into account the shapes of leaves and plants and aim for a contrast so that the eye travels up and down.

All gardens are more effective if they have a focal point, so include one brightly colored pot or some flowering herbs, such as nasturtiums.

Plants for Year-round Interest

In the spring such plants can include primroses. Plant them at eye level, and grow some evergreens for winter color and form, the sweet bay (*Laurus nobilis*) is a great favourite, or some clipped box edging.

Designing with Fruit Containers

Growing fruit in containers requires care and dedication, but fruit trees more than compensate for the work involved with their spring blossom and fresh fruit of the fall.

Anyone contemplating growing fruit in containers has to consider the shape and design of the garden. Almost without exception, fruit grown in containers needs to be trained against a wall and this requires a framework of wires. It should be looked on as a permanent feature. The only exceptions are fruit trees grown on a roof garden as free-standing pyramids or strawberries grown in individual pots or strawberry planters.

WHAT FRUIT TO GROW

The possibilities differ depending on where you are gardening: on a balcony, patio, roof garden or in a window box. If you want to grow fruit in a window box, you may have to content yourself with some Alpine strawberries in among the other herbs and vegetables.

If you want to grow fruit on a balcony or a patio, your choices will be governed by the exposure and the amount of room available, while a roof garden may attract the sun all day but may lack the warm walls necessary to succeed with the

ABOVE *This glossy leaved 'Gala' apple tree is thriving outdoors in a large pot.*

LEFT *Miniature peach trees have been developed that will produce normal-sized fruit in a small container garden.*

tender stone fruits such as apricots, peaches or nectarines.

If you cannot offer a warm wall and your patio faces east or north then the options are more limited. Morello cherries that flourish on a north wall are one choice and a number of the hardier apples which resist late frosts may well fruit on walls with an eastern exposure, although they are unlikely to yield as copiously as they would given a sunnier position. Pears flower earlier than apples and are less resistant to late frosts so at the best they will need a south-eastern wall. A number of plums, particularly the favorite Victoria, will yield good fruit without too much sun if they can be sheltered in early spring from late frosts.

In colder areas some of the hybrid berries or currant bushes, particularly blackcurrants or gooseberries, are more likely to succeed than stone fruit, for they prefer some shade. However, if you do try to grow fruit on a very shaded patio don't persist if the tree or bush fails to flower and produce within three years.

LEFT *Bunches of grapes hang from this healthy vine growing in a warm spot in a large terracotta pot.*

Designing with Fruit Containers

RIGHT *Nothing can beat the taste of home-grown apples, eaten straight from the tree.*

POLLINATION

When you have chosen the fruit you want to grow, check whether the variety is self-fertile or whether you need to grow two trees to pollinate each other. Check the directory entries for guidance.

DWARF TREES

Make the most of any fruit tree that you plant. Dwarf trees will provide punctuation marks on a patio or roof garden and are excellent for growing on balconies. Citrus fruit, oranges and lemons make excellent house plants and can be placed outside in summer for their flowers and fruit. If you have the space and want to grow a free-standing tree one possibility is to plant one or more of the modern dwarf fruit trees in a large container, and use them as the centre of attraction in the garden. Minarette trees grow upright on a single stem and will eventually reach a height of 6–8 ft (1.8–2.4 m). They can be planted as closely as 2 ft (60 cm) apart and therefore 2 or 3 trees can be grown together in a large container. They do need staking, especially if the patio or roof garden is subject to gusts of wind. If you have a favorable position then apples and pears

LEFT *Lemon trees make good container plants on a warm patio. They flower and fruit at the same time and can be brought indoors to overwinter.*

ABOVE *Blackcurrants are easy to grow in containers and flourish in cooler conditions. They can be trained against a wall to take up less room.*

small oranges and lemons, or some of the small lemon trees. They need a minimum winter temperature of 50°F (10°C) and can be put outside in the summer after a period of acclimatization.

STRAWBERRIES

Containers are particularly suitable for growing strawberries and there are a number of special planters available that can be used. The best is the traditional strawberry barrel but the tower pots add height and variety to a patio design and can be used imaginatively to grow pyramids of plants each one dripping with bright red fruit.

ABOVE LEFT *Strawberry pots come in various shapes and sizes. They need additional feeding and watering if they are to produce really good crops.*

can be grown together and they will provide a display of delicate blossom in the spring and contrasting red, yellow and green fruit as they ripen in fall.

CITRUS FRUIT

Container fruit trees don't need to be confined to fruit that remains outside all year. Many a patio is brightened by small trees of citrus fruits, oranges and lemons that can be put outside in the summer and brought inside in winter where they can be treated as house plants. If you want the luxury of growing lemon and orange trees in containers then the most suitable varieties, if space is at a premium, are the x *Citrofortunella* varieties of

TRAINING FRUIT TREES AGAINST WALLS

If you are planning to grow fruit trees in containers you have to measure the amount of wall space available. Fruit trees take up less room when trained against a wall and the delicate stone fruit will flower and fruit better given the warmth and protection of a south- or south-west-facing wall. Fruit trees are usually trained in four shapes, cordon, double cordon (U-shaped), fan, usually used for stone fruit, such as apricots and peaches, and espalier for apples and pears. Cordon-trained trees occupy the least space, about 6 ft (1.8 m) by 4 ft (1.2 m), while a fan-trained tree might require three times this amount depending on the rootstock. Check the directory section to see the space requirements for each fruit.

Designing with Vegetable Containers

Growing vegetables successfully in containers requires thought, planning and care: list the vegetables you prefer and assess the yield, the time they take to mature, and the space available.

Start by listing the vegetables that you want to grow in order of preference to provide a basis for action. This may need to be modified depending on the available space and exposure.

Make a note of the final dimensions of the mature plants, the color, the planting date in a calendar year, the length of time the vegetable takes to mature, and the estimated time of harvest

This plan can be adjusted so that crops are grown to mature over a longer period and certain other vegetables can then be added to prolong the growing season of the container garden. With care it is surprising how many vegetables can be grown in a relatively small space.

THE IMPORTANCE OF TIMING

Time is one of the great priorities. Many vegetables take months to mature. Some brassicas, for example, require 36 weeks in the ground, others as long as 44 weeks. Conversely spring radishes will be ready for eating in 3–6 weeks and most lettuces in 6–8. You may need to compromise. It

TOP *The deep purple of eggplants adds color to any vegetable garden. They need a hot, sheltered position to flower and fruit at their best.*

ABOVE *Vegetables are not just dull green plants stuck away in a corner of the garden. Young lettuces can make an attractive display in the right container.*

may be necessary to abandon Brussels sprouts or late purple-sprouting broccoli in favor of quickly maturing calabrese. The choice will depend on personal preference, the space available and whether it is worth devoting room in the summer to a vegetable that will not be mature until the fall.

DESIGN AND PLANTING

There are two main approaches to planting. You can intermingle a number of vegetables in a container to give a contrast of color and form. (Take care to see that more vigorous plants do not overshadow smaller ones.) Alternatively, plant in blocks, devoting one container to each vegetable. If you have sufficient containers this simple approach looks attractive with bold blocks of color.

Include vegetables with colorful foliage, such as beets or ruby chard; the bright red and dark green of their leaves brings out the paler greens of other vegetables such as lettuces and young carrots. Think of the different greens and the shapes of different crops. Look at photographs of traditional vegetable gardens to see which vegetables look attractive grown together.

Containers can be moved around throughout the year as crops mature, are harvested, and then replaced. Give each container as much light as possible and see that growing plants do not cast too much shade.

BELOW *Bush tomatoes do not require staking. They do best if grown in large pots. Feed them regularly.*

25

Designing with Vegetable Containers

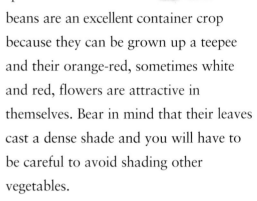

RIGHT The dense heads of a traditional Savoy cabbage look good anywhere.

BELOW Patio furniture can be painted in contrasting colors. This choice emphasizes the purple hanging eggplants.

THE VERTICAL DIMENSION

A number of vegetables can be grown for their height, which adds a vertical dimension to the garden. Runner beans are particularly useful, and a number of tender vegetables, such as tomatoes, cucumbers and peppers, can also be grown up canes.

Jerusalem artichokes and runner beans grow upward and provide changing levels which add interest to a small space. Scarlet runner beans are an excellent container crop because they can be grown up a teepee and their orange-red, sometimes white and red, flowers are attractive in themselves. Bear in mind that their leaves cast a dense shade and you will have to be careful to avoid shading other vegetables.

Another idea is to grow blocks of baby vegetables in individual containers. Seed companies have developed new varieties that are excellent for the container garden.

GROWING TENDER VEGETABLES OUTSIDE

The principle of growing vegetables on supports can be extended to a number of the more unusual vegetables that can be grown outside in milder regions given a hot, sunny position. They include eggplants, zucchini, cucumbers, peppers and tomatoes, as well as pumpkins.

If you wish, you can specialize in these vegetables. They can be grown on supports and add unusual colors to the container garden as well as bringing different tastes to the kitchen. Study their requirements carefully. They will need to be tied to the supports and watered regularly to grow successfully.

BABY VEGETABLES

Many vegetables taste better when they are harvested at a young age. These include carrots, turnips and kohl rabi, but the seed companies have now developed a number of baby vegetables that can be grown conveniently in groups in containers. An example of this type of vegetable would be the cauliflower 'Idol' that can be sown in early spring and harvested twelve weeks later when the heads are no bigger than a tennis ball. Baby varieties of all the popular vegetables are available, meaning that baby parsnips and sweet corn can be considered as choices. Many seed catalogs list these baby vegetables separately and they should be included in the vegetable container garden as a matter of course.

EXPOSURE AND LONGEVITY

It is important to consider the exposure of the container garden. Most vegetables do best in an open sunny position, but there are a number, such as Swiss chard, lettuce and carrots, that will grow well in partial shade.

Bear in mind that some vegetables are over and done with fairly quickly; a cauliflower or cabbage produces just one head on a plant, while other plants provide a continuous crop over a long period; for example Swiss chard or ruby chard produce more leaves the more leaves you pick.

SMALL SPACES

Vegetables can be grown effectively in very small spaces. Just because the only space available is a window box does not mean that you cannot grow vegetables, but in such a small space you really do need to grow a mixture. An assortment of vegetables and fruit, such as two tomato plants, two or three strawberry plants, some lettuces and miniature cabbages, can easily be planted in a standard window box and this looks attractive during the summer months as the vegetables mature. Parsley and chives can also be added for variety.

BELOW *Galvanized steel containers planted with the cabbage 'January King' make a good color contrast with catmint (Nepeta). Other flowering herbs can be grouped with vegetables to make contrasting color schemes.*

Patios

A well thought-out patio garden can be a delight. Make a list of the plants you wish to grow and then plan the position of each container, checking that the colors will blend well.

A patio is the most sensible, easiest and most convenient place to site a container kitchen garden. In many houses the kitchen door leads directly to it, and the cook can step just outside to harvest the herbs and vegetables that grow on the patio.

It is important to consider the size and uses for the patio. Is it just a passageway between house and garden that needs to

ABOVE Sunflowers grow quickly, do well in containers and provide a burst of color on a sunny patio.

TENDER PLANTS

A warm sunny patio enables the gardener to grow a number of tender plants, provided they can be taken indoors during the cold months of the year. Oranges and lemons are particularly suitable and there are some varieties that will not grow too large. They carry white scented flowers from spring to summer and the fruit is borne at the same time. As well as the traditional citrus fruits small forms of satsumas and the dwarf Chinese orange are also available.

be kept clear, or is it used as a seating area, furnished with tables and chairs for eating out? Is it surrounded by walls up which you can grow peas or scarlet runner beans, and is it large enough for you to grow some small fruit trees in large containers? Can you design a planting scheme that pleases the eye?

PLAN WITH CARE

Plan ruthlessly. Place your containers carefully so that they form pleasing, harmonious groups of differing shapes and sizes. Use containers with different textures and materials and then plant so that the smallest plants are in the front and the tallest at the back to hide unsightly walls.

LEFT *The patio doesn't need to be crammed with containers. Allow space to sit among the plants and enjoy them in summer when they are at their best.*

Establish any permanent plants first. If you have a patio that attracts a large amount of sunshine then you may want to consider growing some fruit trees, especially the delicate stone fruit with pink blossoms in spring. Once in position a large container filled with potting soil is a very heavy object to move.

ABOVE *A delightful corner of a patio with a decorative chair painted to contrast with the lemon tree and clipped box in tubs.*

Roof Gardens

Roof gardens are the ultimate city garden. They can be grand, or as simple as a cottage garden, they may just have a few containers, or harbor plants in great profusion. The best are extraordinary.

Roof gardens are the ultimate in container gardening but they have their own set of problems.

The first and most important consideration, whether the roof garden is large or small, is the weight of the plants and containers. Full containers are fairly heavy and it is essential that the roof is strong enough to bear the load. It is sensible to have the load-bearing capacity of your roof checked by a structural engineer before starting work on creating your rooftop oasis.

A roof is also exposed and screens may need to be erected to provide both shelter and seclusion. Get professional help when doing this. If screens and plants are not absolutely secure, there is the risk that they might blow down in a high wind, possibly causing damage to property or injury to people below.

FLOORING AND WATERING

A roof garden also requires flooring. It is a good idea to keep this as light as possible to avoid increasing the weight. Wooden boards, light tiles and gravel are all worth considering. Finally, almost the most important aspect of a roof garden is watering. Any roof garden must have an easily accessible supply of water and

LEFT *Even in the heart of the city, containers can be used to create an oasis of color and tranquility.*

there is a strong case for installing an automatic watering system. At the least have an outside tap available. Be careful not to interfere with the roof drainage when installing flooring or containers.

THE DESIGN OF ROOF GARDENS

Large roof gardens should be planned as a series of rooms, each area contributing a different aspect. A kitchen roof garden might form one of these rooms. You can grow free-standing trees, and pyramid apples and plums can be grown without the need to train them against a wall.

WATCH THE DETAILS

Try to consider every detail of your garden. Conceal growbags, hiding them within specially constructed troughs, and concentrate on cultivating the smaller vegetables and herbs because they are neater in habit. A mini-potager of baby vegetables in matching containers is a good idea.

The garden can be divided by containers at different levels or with trellis or arches. Vines can even be trained to cover a pergola with a canopy of foliage.

BELOW *A sitting area on a roof garden decorated with sweet-smelling tobacco plants and the lovely blue* agapanthus *in tubs.*

Window Boxes

Window boxes are the first garden for many people and are among the most popular and appreciated of all forms of gardening. They add color and decoration everywhere.

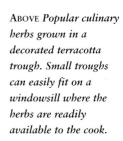

Attractive window boxes are probably more appreciated than any other form of container gardening. They brighten city streets, embellish housing estates and often display marvellous ingenuity of color that takes an enormous amount of time and care to achieve.

Growing vegetables successfully in a window box demands all this, but you can be certain of excellent results that will astonish everyone if you take sufficient care of the plants and water and feed them on a regular basis.

PRACTICAL CONSIDERATIONS

There are a number of practical things to consider. First of all the window box must fit beneath the window where it is to be placed. Then it must be securely fastened in position.

When it is full of plants and potting soil, a window box is fairly heavy. Anyone planning a window box overhanging a busy street must be certain that it is held firmly in place.

The box must also blend in with the building. Window boxes are normally made of wood or plastic and can be painted to match the color of the trim around the window.

The window box must be able to drain freely. The bottom must have a number of drainage holes and if it is placed flat on a windowsill then it should be supported on wood or clay blocks to allow free drainage.

ABOVE *Popular culinary herbs grown in a decorated terracotta trough. Small troughs can easily fit on a windowsill where the herbs are readily available to the cook.*

LEFT *A variety of kitchen herbs including some purple-leaved basil, chives, parsley and mint grown in a trough that can be moved inside when required.*

WATERING AND FEEDING

Plants in a window box need watering frequently, and feeding at least once every two weeks. They do not contain a large amount of potting soil so plants growing in them need additional encouragement in order to flourish.

PLANTS FOR WINDOW BOXES

The most obvious window box plants are herbs, especially if the window faces south or west. They can be mixed with a few strawberry plants for fruit in the summer and some small bush tomato plants can be included. If the box is fed and watered regularly then they will all yield a reasonable crop. Other good salad plants include lettuces or baby carrots whose roots do not require any great depth of soil or some of the baby vegetables that mature quickly.

If you prefer to look at flowers rather than green vegetables, you can plant a number of flowering herbs. A good number are suitable, including chives that flower in early summer, and the colorful nasturtiums that flower at the end. Grow plants that mature quickly and change the contents of the box frequently with the seasons.

BELOW *Ornamental kales flanked by cyclamen and pots of winter heather make an arresting display on a windowsill.*

Balconies

Balconies are romantic and the gardener who designs a planting for a balcony should try and achieve an air of mystery. They should be suitable trysting places.

ABOVE RIGHT Balconies deserve pots that complement their air of mystery and romance; terracotta and lead containers are both ideal.

Balconies are elegant, whether they are terraces running around the upper floors of a house, small individual rooms framed with wrought-iron outside picture windows, or miniature roof gardens backed on one side by the walls of a building. Usually they are highly visible and the container kitchen gardener has to take special care to ensure that the planting scheme pleases the eye.

GROW CLIMBING PLANTS

Generally balconies need climbing plants to hide the walls. These can either be annuals, such as scarlet runner beans, or perennial climbers, such as climbing roses or the golden hop, or alternatively the walls can be partially hidden by hanging baskets or wall pots.

If you want a permanent evergreen covering, it will be necessary to plant one

RIGHT Decorative pots on a formal terrace give the balcony interest and can be used to prolong the flowering season in a garden. Here the red fuchsia plants draw attention to the stone balustrade and the ornamented terracotta adds a contrasting texture.

of the many available ivies. Other ever-green climbers include the variegated *Griselinia*, or the sweet-scented Chinese jasmine, *Trachelospermum*. Pots and troughs all need to be grouped carefully because they will be seen at close range and the planting must echo the style of the building.

FORMAL AND INFORMAL PLANTINGS

If the balcony is an old-fashioned formal one with wrought-iron railings, a rampant cottage-style of vegetable planting would be inappropriate. Instead, the gardener should plan something like formal clipped conifers in tubs with small orange or lemon trees placed out of doors in summer. Other herbs, including rosemary and lavender, can be trained in a formal fashion. These will provide a pleasant scent in spring and summer as well as attractive foliage.

If the balcony is more private, the planting can be informal and consist of groups of herbs and vegetables grown in tubs. Try a number of flowering herbs, such as the sweet-smelling pelargoniums with tomato plants or peppers that you train up the walls.

PLAN SOME TRAILING PLANTS

It is also a good idea to utilize the front of the balcony to grow trailing plants that will hang over the edges. This looks

attractive. Nasturtiums will provide good color in the late summer and there are a number of trailing, miniature tomatoes that give good color and red fruit in summer.

Grape vines, too, are attractive trailing plants and grow well in containers. If they are trained along the balcony in the spring, the leaves contribute a lovely fresh green in summer and dark orange and red fall tints. The black and green grapes are useful fruit for eating or home-made wine.

ABOVE A simple, unfussy color scheme of white and purple blends in well with the painted railings and gives a clean, modern feel to this wooden balcony.

Doorways and Steps

Containers framing a doorway or punctuating a formal flight of steps have to be planned with great care. They set the style of the house and make an important statement.

ABOVE RIGHT A broad, shallow pot of mixed herbs can sit on the back step where it is easily accessible.

OPPOSITE Low-growing pots of mixed herbs can be used symmetrically on steps to frame an entrance. They are quite easy to plant and maintain.

Containers used to frame a doorway or line a flight of steps have to be planned with great care. A front doorway announces the style of the house and should be both welcoming and decorative. Many doors are framed by pruned shrubs or trees grown as standards. This can give a severe impression but the tubs can be brightened up in the winter with ornamental kales interspersed with winter pansies or evergreen boughs that celebrate the season. Other choices might include dwarf evergreens that are easy to grow in containers, or tubs of citrus trees. The citruses will need shelter in the winter in colder climates.

DECORATING STAIRWAYS

If the doorway is approached by a flight of steps, each step can be decorated by matching pots with displays of low-growing herbs that can be changed with the season. If the steps connect the house with another level in the garden, they too can be decorated with containers. Match the style of the container to the steps. Weathered terracotta and bricks go well together and each pot can be planted with an individual herb.

If the flight of steps is grander and leads, for instance, from a semi-basement area to an upper terrace, the steps should be punctuated with matching decorative pots, in keeping with the house. These can be planted with a mixture of herbs or vegetables. Try to preserve some symmetry and make a definite statement about the design of the garden, showing that you have thought about it.

RIGHT Clipped bay trees in Versailles tubs painted to match the front door make a classic statement.

container
Gardening
basics

The basics of container gardening are the same as for any other form of gardening. Seeds are sown, plants grow, mature and are harvested. The cycle of birth and rebirth is eternal. Plants in containers, however, are more confined. Their roots are restricted and they need more nourishment as a result. They also need more care when it comes to watering. This is the really big difference between container gardening and "gardening in the raw." Containers dry out, especially in summer. Watering all containers at least once a day in hot weather is an essential; without it the plants will not survive.

LEFT *A mixed terracotta pot of low-growing herbs is the first essential for any serious cook. Try to grow a selection of herbs with differing leaf colors as the varying greens provide their own quiet attraction.*

Choosing Containers – *pots and troughs*

The most important thing when choosing containers is to ensure that they fit in with their surroundings. Another is cost – handmade terracotta is expensive, but a search of junk or antique shops may produce worthwhile trophies for little money.

Whatever style of pots you choose, make sure that they will look good together. If you plan an extensive container garden, you will need containers of various shapes and sizes for large and small plants. If they are to be grouped, the groupings must match. One of the most popular materials is terracotta, with pots available in many shapes and sizes. Many of the designs are copies of Victorian styles which were available in the 19th century, and some of the more elaborate urns are based on classical designs. If you do not like the rather raw orange-brown colour of new cheap pots, you can tone them down by painting them in soft colors. Alternatively,

Most containers are made from terracotta, literally "baked earth." New pots can be painted or aged to look good in any area.

Terracotta pot 10 in (25 cm) high

Terracotta pots 4 in (10 cm), 6 in (15 cm), 8 in (20 cm), and 9 in (23 cm) in diameter

Terracotta egg pot 14 in (35 cm)diameter 14 in (35 cm) high

Ali Baba jar 15 in (38 cm) in diameter, 20 in (50 cm) high

Terracotta pot with glazed rim 12¹⁄₂ in (32 cm) in diameter, 11 in (28 cm) high

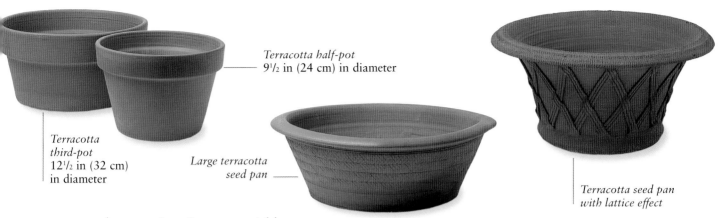

Terracotta half-pot
9¹/₂ in (24 cm) in diameter

Terracotta
third-pot
12¹/₂ in (32 cm)
in diameter

Large terracotta
seed pan

Terracotta seed pan
with lattice effect

encourage them to "age" more quickly by painting them in yogurt or a mixture of sour milk and yogurt. This attracts algae. Within just a few weeks, they will give the pot a pleasant greenish patina.

TROUGHS AND BASINS

A container garden with pots only would look somewhat dull, so it is worthwhile incorporating a number of troughs. The most expensive and heaviest are made from lead but there are now many designs manufactured from fibreglass or stone. You can also use kitchen sinks and stone troughs.

Always position large pots, urns and troughs before filling and planting them; once full, they may be too heavy to move. Place the empty pots where you think you would like them to go, then move them around, trying out different arrangements until you are satisfied they fit the space before you fill them.

Terracotta "long Toms"
5 in (12.5 cm), 7 in
(17.5 cm), and 9 in
(23 cm) in diameter

Terracotta swag
pot (plain)
16 in (40 cm)
in diameter,
13 in (33 cm) high

Peachstone trough
18 x 11 x 9 in
(45 x 28 x 23 cm)

Lead trough
29 x 10 in (74 x 25 cm)

Choosing Containers –
wall pots and hanging baskets

*Container gardens can be extended upward to
great effect using wall pots and hanging baskets.
They can be planted to paint an abstract picture.*

The container gardener can extend the number of plants and the growing area by using a variety of wall pots attached to available walls and hanging baskets on pergolas. These are especially useful for planting on balconies where it is unlikely that there will be room for raised beds to accommodate climbers to cover walls or trellises.

USING WALL POTS
The most attractive wall pots are made in terracotta with flat backs. They come in various shapes and designs and groups of these can be positioned on a wall, planted to paint an abstract picture. These can be filled with herbs or vegetables, such as bush beans, or better still, trailing tomatoes that will hang over the edge of the pot. They are not suitable for all plants, and planning and planting must be undertaken with care. If they are used for vegetables they must be placed low

*Metal filigree
hanging basket
13$\frac{1}{2}$ in (34 cm)
in diameter*

*"Honey-pot" style
_____ wall pot*

*Terracotta
wall pot _____*

*Terracotta lattice-
effect wall pot*

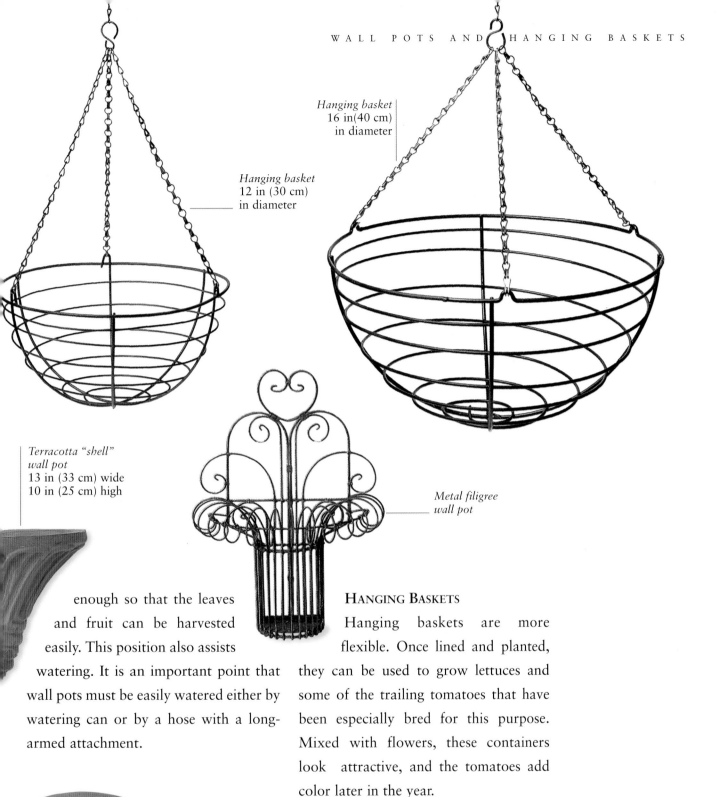

Hanging basket
16 in (40 cm)
in diameter

Hanging basket
12 in (30 cm)
in diameter

*Terracotta "shell"
wall pot*
13 in (33 cm) wide
10 in (25 cm) high

*Metal filigree
wall pot*

*Terracotta
wall pot*
10 in (25 cm) wide
8 in (20 cm) high

enough so that the leaves and fruit can be harvested easily. This position also assists watering. It is an important point that wall pots must be easily watered either by watering can or by a hose with a long-armed attachment.

HANGING BASKETS

Hanging baskets are more flexible. Once lined and planted, they can be used to grow lettuces and some of the trailing tomatoes that have been especially bred for this purpose. Mixed with flowers, these containers look attractive, and the tomatoes add color later in the year.

Planting hanging baskets is not nearly as difficult as it might appear. They should be planted in late spring although they need protection overnight if there is any threat of frost.

Homemade Containers – *window boxes and troughs*

Very often the correct size of trough or window box is difficult to find. Tailor-made wooden boxes are easy to make and a good solution.

It is often difficult to find containers to fit a particular space. Windowsills may be too large or too small for the boxes you can buy. Balconies may require larger boxes than those you can find if the overall design is to be maintained, or you may not like the design of the individual planters available. One solution is to make your own containers. A range of containers can be made quite simply from wood or particle board. With care and proper treatment, they will provide long service.

You can also make a number of wooden containers, such as troughs and Versailles tubs, in various shapes and designs that fit the style of the garden. Most good garden woodworking manuals contain a number of design ideas that you can adapt to what you need.

ABOVE *A slatted wooden trough provides a rustic look that fits in with a number of design schemes.*

PAINTING A WOODEN TROUGH

1 There are a number of wood stains available in a range of colors that are safe to use with plants. Here a wooden trough has been painted with bright blue wood stain. Rub it down lightly with fine sandpaper when dry.

2 This trough is being given a distressed finish. A light coat of terracotta emulsion paint is applied over the blue wood stain. When this has dried it, too, is rubbed down and the two colors blend together.

3 The end result is a gently distressed finish. This technique can be adopted to whatever color scheme you choose. The paint can be sealed with a matt varnish and this provides added protection against the elements.

WOODEN BOXES

There are many good books available that give advice on constructing window boxes and troughs for the garden. The projects vary in complexity and the number of tools that are required. If you plan to make a number of boxes for a special situation, it is worthwhile to purchase good quality woodworking tools because they make any job of this type much easier.

Measure everything carefully. Nothing is more irritating than building a box for a windowsill and finding that it is fractionally too small, or worse still, too large. Use substantial, thick wood or particle board. It should be at least ¾ in (19 mm) thick. Make sure that the corners and bottom are properly secured.

Either buy a routing tool that enables you to make grooved joints or secure the sides and bottom to battens so that the box is rigid and firm.

Don't just bang a nail or a screw through from one board into another and expect the box to last.

ABOVE *Bright blue painted tins can be used as simple containers that blend in with any decorative scheme. Calendulas in varying shades of yellow and orange make a color contrast. Punch holes in the bottoms.*

WICKER TROUGH WITH STRAWBERRIES

1 Staple a polythene liner inside a wicker basket and then line it with a layer of sphagnum moss to retain the moisture and hide the polythene. Press this firmly around all the edges.

2 Fill the basket with good potting soil, then plant the strawberries firmly in the basket. Two plants are sufficient in a basket of this size. Don't forget that strawberries are greedy plants and need feeding.

3 The basket can be placed outside or on a shelf or windowsill. Water and feed them throughout the growing season. The plants will grow and fill the container and the fruit will hang down above the ground.

Homemade Containers – *window boxes and troughs*

ABOVE *Strawberries planted in a raised bed can be protected by a covering of straw.*

CHECK THE DESIGN

Make sure that the window box fits in well with the window and looks right in position. This also applies to planters that stand on their own on patios or balconies, such as Versailles tubs or wooden boxes. You should treat all wood with horticulturally recommended preservative, following the instructions on the label, and paying particular attention to the cut edges. Drill holes in the base to allow the container to drain and line it with thick polythene that can be stapled in place with a staple gun. Make drainage holes in the polyethene and check that these align with the holes in the base of the container.

RAISED BEDS

If you have a larger patio, you may want to build some raised beds. These allow you to grow larger and more substantial plants, such as fruit trees and shrubs. They are also a great help to gardeners who cannot reach the ground easily.

Pay attention to the design and think carefully about the final result before you start. There may be room for small, free-standing beds in the middle of a terrace or roof garden that allow all-round access, and two small beds may look better than one large one.

Raised beds can be built out of brick, decorative blocks, or concrete slabs that can then be rendered and painted.

BUILDING A RAISED BED

1 Making a raised bed is an excellent addition to a patio if there is sufficient room. Mark out the area with string and then dig out a trench 12 in (30 cm) wide and 12 in (30 cm) deep. Fill this footing with concrete.

2 Leave the concrete over night and then start building the inner wall using cinder blocks. Each block is laid on a ½ in (12 mm) layer of mortar with one end "butted" with a triangular dab of mortar. Check the level.

3 Build the outer walls out from each corner. When you have laid three or four courses of bricks set a string guideline between the two corners and infill with bricks inserting metal wall ties at intervals.

4 When the walls are finished lay a top layer of bricks lengthways across both the outer and inner walls. Fill the base of the bed with stones or other drainage material and then fill with good potting soil.

LEFT *This raised bed has been carefully designed to be a work of art. The profusion of contrasting heights, widths, leaf sizes, colors and shapes has created an edible tapestry.*

Choose the material to fit in with the surroundings. Natural materials, particularly wood and brick, always look attractive but most surfaces can be painted to blend in better with the surrounding space.

If the raised bed is to be built on a solid surface such as a patio, check that the base is broken up so that the container can drain freely; otherwise it will become waterlogged.

You can have raised beds built professionally or build them yourself (see opposite).

UNUSUAL CONTAINERS

Painted old car tires make unusual containers for all plants and are often used for planting potatoes. Add a base to the lowest tire, ensuring that there is sufficient drainage, then pile the others on top.

Choosing Containers –
larger plants

If you plan to grow large trees or shrubs, you need an equally large container. It must be in proportion with the plant and must blend in with the design of your garden.

There are a number of things to think about when considering large containers. Many large plants, trees and fruiting shrubs will need as large a container as you can provide if they are to flourish and attain anywhere near their potential size.

Larger plants grow best in raised beds or in special large containers chosen so that they fit in with the overall design of the garden. Even large containers need to have some drainage at the bottom. An automatic watering system is of great assistance in keeping the plants moist.

MATCH THE CONTAINER TO THE PLANT
Try to match the style of the container to the style of the plant. Trees or shrubs with a spreading habit look best in wide-brimmed pots. Very often large containers are made from terracotta, but other materials, such as stone or glazed earthenware, are also suitable provided they can accommodate the root system of the plant. Keep the containers and their contents in proportion. It is always

ABOVE *Replicas of classical urns and pots are available at many garden centers. They are excellent for formal gardens.*

RIGHT *A clipped rosemary bush, trained into a ball. Training rosemary is complicated and has to be carried out carefully over a period of years.*

possible to transplant a tree as it grows into a larger container; any small plant alone in a large pot will look bare and isolated. It is best to fill in the space around the main plant with low-growing herbs or small vegetables because this will keep the planting in proportion.

BARRELS AND TALL POTS

Half barrels make good containers and can accommodate quite large trees. They look natural and fit in with almost any surrounding. You may be able to find old barrels in a junk shop or scrap yard or ask at a garden supply store.

Tall pots sometimes make excellent features on a patio garden. Ali Baba pots are very decorative on their own and hardly need to be filled with plants. If you are planning to use a very tall pot, be careful. There are few plants that work well in really big containers. Choose some trailing nasturtiums or something equally simple.

Very large containers need to be placed carefully in the garden and particular care has to be taken over the background. The design of a garden is composed of many things; the background color is very often forgotten.

RIGHT This is an excellent example of achieving different levels on a patio with a variety of containers, large and small.

Basic Equipment

Basic equipment for a container garden is relatively simple. No lawnmower is required, nor is a spade, fork or rake. Buy the best hand tools and they will last a lifetime.

Gloves
Light gardening gloves are a great help

The small scale of a container garden means that there is no need for a large selection of specialist garden tools. Even a garden fork and spade are surplus to requirements, although a spade might come in useful for filling containers with soil mix or shovelling sand and cement during building operations.

BUY THE BEST

When it comes to garden tools the rule is to buy the best you can afford and keep them clean and in good condition. They will repay this small amount of care with years of service. As a minimum the container gardener needs the following:
Secateurs: for pruning and training trees and shrubs. They can also be used to cut herbs and flowers. Bypass secateurs with replacable blades are the most popular.

Hand fork and hand trowel: for transplanting and weeding. Buy the best stainless steel if you can afford it. This might make a good suggestion for a special birthday present. Narrow trowels are the most useful because you can dig out a deeper narrower hole more easily with them without disturbing other plants in

Sieve – non essential

Galvanized metal watering can

Fine-spray rose

Extension

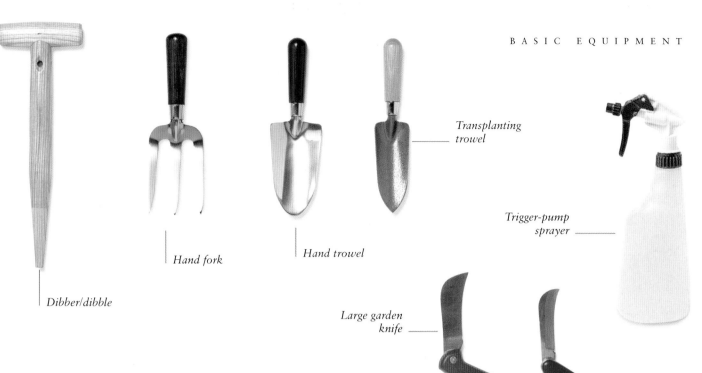

Transplanting trowel

Hand fork

Hand trowel

Trigger-pump sprayer

Dibber/dibble

Large garden knife

Pruning knife

the containers. A hand fork is also helpful for loosening compacted soil mix and weeding in the summer. Even on a roof garden weeds will arrive unwelcome on the city breeze.

Dibber: a good tool for making holes for small plants. Leeks are always planted with a dibber, and it is useful for brassicas and other vegetables.

Hand rake: this is essential. A miniature cultivating rake smooths over the surface of the potting soil and helps to remove old leaves and weeds. It can also be used to make furrows when planting seeds.

Hand shears (optional): you will only need this tool if you have large plants that you need to trim in summer or fall.

Garden knife: for cutting pieces of string and raffia, cutting off the tops of carrots and other garden uses.

Pruning knife and saw (optional): you only need a pruning saw if a branch is too large to be severed manually. You can usually prune everything you need with a good pair of secateurs.

Watering can: get a good quality watering can with a long spout to reach the back of containers.

Sprayer: one of the smaller spray units will be all that is required.

Additionally: wire, vine eyes, hammer, bolts, ring eyes, screws and various nails, for a wire frame.

Propagating unit (optional): you will only need this if you sow a number of seeds and take cuttings regularly.

"Garden Snipper"

Secateurs/pruning shears (medium)

Hand shears (optional)

Preparing the Site

Check on the final stages of the container garden before the pots, soil mix and gravel for drainage are delivered. Make everything as perfect as possible.

ABOVE RIGHT Weathered terracotta pots have almost the same status as antiques and are extremely sought-after. The large tin mug is an excellent accompaniment.

Once the containers have been chosen, the garden designed, any raised beds built, window boxes constructed and fixed, the containers have to be delivered, positioned, and planted.

Before this the final preparations to the site have to be made – the last touches in transferring the garden design from paper onto the ground.

WATERING

Regardless of the system you plan to adopt you must ensure that there is adequate provision of water to the site and that it is easily available. This may involve installing an outside tap. The plumbing for this should be done before the containers arrive.

FLOORING

A terrace or roof garden may have to have new floors laid of gravel, wooden boards, brick or decorative paving. Do this when any permanent containers, such as raised beds, are in place. Take care that the design and materials match the house and surroundings. Try to avoid a bare patch of concrete.

PREPARING A WOODEN BARREL FOR PLANTING

1 Barrels need soaking before you start to make them watertight. Fill the barrel with water and leave it overnight or plunge it in a tub.

2 Lay the barrel on its side to dry off any surplus water. Remember you will need drainage holes in the bottom of the barrel and it should be lined with plastic.

3 Fit the liner into the barrel and make certain that there are holes in the base that match the holes in the bottom of the barrel. Add the gravel.

4 When you have added a good layer of gravel fill the barrel with mix and plant. Trim off the plastic and secure it with staples. Water thoroughly.

CONTAINERS

When the containers arrive, group them and change the design around until you are completely satisfied that they are in the right place. At this point you may find that they are not exactly level. It is a good idea to raise them off the ground on special feet. This helps pots to drain more freely and is important for any window boxes where accumulated water may rot a wooden sill.

WIRE FRAMEWORK AND TRELLIS

When the final position of the containers has been fixed and your planting plan is clear, you may want to erect a wire framework on which to train fruit trees. You will need a mortar drill, plastic molly bolts, screw eyes and tensioning bolts as well as strong 2–3 mm wire. Attach the wires horizontally 15–18 in (38–45 cm) apart.

You may wish to put up a trellis. Erecting a stout trellis is easy enough on a patio when it can usually be attached to an existing fence or wall. If you are putting up a fence of any sort around a roof garden it is essential to ensure that it is absolutely secure and there is no danger of it blowing away and causing damage or injury in a high wind. Unless you are an accomplished handyman it is better to employ a building professional for this job.

Finally, order the appropriate soil mix for the plants you are planning to grow and sufficient gravel to put at the base of the pots to give adequate drainage.

PLANTING LARGE SEEDS

1 Choose a large container and add a good layer of gravel to the bottom to provide adequate drainage. Add multi-purpose soil mix up to the height at which the seeds will be sown.

2 Space out the seeds to the correct distance and then cover them with multi-purpose potting soil, to the depth indicated on the seed packet. Water the container well and allow to drain.

PLANTING HANGING BASKETS

1 Line a hanging basket with a good layer of sphagnum moss, packing the moss tightly around the sides. Put a plastic liner inside the moss and cut holes for the plants.

2 Fill the liner with special moisture-retaining potting soil and then push the plants through the liner and moss from the inside. Firm the mix well around the roots. Water well.

Choosing and Buying Container Plants

Make a list of all the plants that you want to grow and stick to it. Remember that plants get bigger, don't worry if the containers look a bit bare when first planted, they will soon fill out.

The most important thing to consider when growing any plant in a container is the direction of the sun. In the northern hemisphere, if a patio faces south, is sheltered, and the general climate is hot enough, heat-loving plants can be grown. If it faces north then you should concentrate on those plants that will flourish in a degree of shade. Lists of suitable plants are given on pages 154–5.

It is important to plan purchasing and planting carefully. Make a list of the plants that you plan to grow and then check whether there is a specialist nursery near you. If there is, you can purchase the plants you require in person. However, you may have to order them to be sent by mail. Nurseries are well used to sending plants through the post and it is seldom that plants arrive in anything other than good condition.

It is best to buy from a specialist, rather than from a general garden center or supermarket where the choice may be limited and, usually, no specialist advice or help is available.

BARE-ROOT PLANTS

Plants should be planted at the right time of the year and this applies particularly to trees and shrubs. In the south, these are best planted in the fall when the growth

ABOVE *A large herb garden has the room to grow large clumps of herbs with contrasting leaf colors. Purple-leaved sage, French lavender and border pinks are all planted here in separate small beds.*

ABOVE *A new plant should have a strong, healthy stem and the leaves should not be discolored or drooping.*

is dying down but the soil remains warm and moist enough so that the root system can grow. Plant in spring in the north. Also, for roses and fruit trees you are better off purchasing bare-root plants rather than container-grown trees and shrubs.

This may sound like strange advice, especially if the plants are to continue in a container garden, but plants raised in containers often have a restricted root system and bare-root plants planted at the right time of the year do better. No reputable supplier would send out bare-root plants at the wrong time of the year.

HEELING IN

If you cannot plant any trees or shrubs as soon as they arrive, dig a small trench in one container, lay the plants in it at an angle of 45° and cover them firmly with soil until you have time to complete the planting properly. They are unlikely to come to too much harm if they are not left for too long. If a frost threatens, protect the plants by covering them with row cover material or some mulch.

BUYING PLANTS IN PERSON

If you plan to buy the plants yourself at a garden center there are a number of things to look out for. Check all the leaves for signs of pests or disease, and make sure that the plant does not suffer

from leaf drop. Avoid plants that have moss growing on the top of the container, as this indicates that they have been there for too long. Check to see that there are not too many roots growing out of the holes at the bottom of the container for the same reason.

Finally, look to see that the plant is healthy and that it has a good shape with equally spaced branches. Remember you may want to turn containers around so that each plant gets an equal share of the light over the year.

ABOVE *A wheelbarrow makes an attractive and unusual focal point in this container herb garden.*

Potting and Repotting

The principles of planting and repotting are the same. Plants need to be firm in the soil mix to prevent air pockets around their roots and have adequate drainage to avoid waterlogging.

All plants grown in containers should be planted the same way. Choose a container 2 in (5 cm) larger than the root-ball of the plant. Remove the plant from the original container and gently tease out the roots if they have become congested. Trim off any damaged roots. Put a good layer of crocks, broken tiles or stones at the bottom of the container and then a layer of soil mix. Put the plant in the container, making certain that the soil level is the same in the new container as it was in the old. Add the mix around the sides of the pot making sure that it is pressed firmly against all the roots. Firm the soil with your hands or a dibber but don't ram it down too tightly. Rap the container down on a hard surface two or three times to shake out any air pockets. Water thoroughly and top up the level with more potting soil as it settles.

ABOVE *Sweet basil is one of the most popular herbs in the kitchen and can easily be grown on a windowsill or put outside in summer.*

POTTING ON

Young plants need to be transferred from small pots to larger pots, depending on their rate of growth. This should be done in stages. Always transfer a growing plant to a pot just larger than the one it is in at present, about 2 in (5 cm) diameter larger is ideal. This keeps the growth at a steady rate. If you potted on into a pot that was considerably larger, the roots would spread out too quickly which upsets the growing balance of the plant.

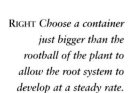

RIGHT *Choose a container just bigger than the rootball of the plant to allow the root system to develop at a steady rate.*

REPOTTING

How often a plant should be repotted is a difficult question to answer. At one end of the scale, repotting may not be possible. Large raised beds, especially when they contain permanent trees or shrubs, cannot easily be emptied. In these cases remove as much of the top mix as possible without damaging the roots of the plant and then replace it with fresh and add a suitable fertilizer. Otherwise, in containers that can be moved the soil mix should be emptied out and replaced every other year, and this should be done every year when the plant is growing vigorously.

PLANTING UP A LARGE SHRUB OR TREE

1 Add stones or broken crocks to the container to provide drainage and then a layer of soil mix. Use a compost-based mix if possible. It contains nutrients for long-term growth.

2 Lower the plant into the container, spread out the roots if they are not too congested and check that the soil is at the same level as in the original container. Check the plant is perpendicular.

3 Add soil mix all round the plant pushing it down firmly with your fingers. Insert a support stake down the side of the pot. Do not push it through the rootball as this damages the roots.

4 Firm the compost. Secure the plant to the stake and top up the soil mix level. If you can, lift up and tap the container down firmly on the ground to eliminate any air pockets.

5 Water the container thoroughly and check that the plant is firm in the pot. Roll the plant gently into position if you have not planted it *in situ* but it is much better to plant the container in its final position as a large container full of soil mix is fairly heavy.

Choosing the Growing Medium

There are three groups of potting soil and a number of special mixes for different plants. For all general gardening, sowing seeds or planting, a good, multi-purpose soil mix is best.

Seedling mixes are specially formulated for growing seeds. They may be loam-based (i.e. contain soil) or be peat-, or peat-substitute-based. They contain few nutrients, are very fine textured so that the seed has close contact with the mix, and retain water well. If seedlings are kept in a seedling mix for any length of time after germination and before pricking out they need additional feeding.

UNIVERSAL (MULTI-PURPOSE) MIXES

These can be used to germinate seedlings and also to pot up a number of plants. They fall in between seedling mix and

PEAT-BASED GROWING MEDIUMS These are made with three main ingredients, peat, or peat substitute, fertilizer and base grit or gravel to add drainage.

potting mix. If you are going to use a multi-purpose mix for pots then you will need to feed more than if you used a normal potting mix but this is only a minor consideration. They are probably the best mixes to buy for general garden work, but they should not be used for containers with large permanent plants.

Peat-based growing medium

Base fertilizer

Peat

Coarse grit (gravel)

SOIL pH TEST

1 ACID
The acidity of the soil is only important in containers if you want to grow acid-loving plants when you need to use an ericaceous (acid) soil mix.

2 NEUTRAL
Most soil mixes are neutral. To test the acidity buy a simple soil-testing kit. Put some soil in a tube with the liquid and shake it. It will change color according to the pH.

3 ALKALINE
Neutral soil is suitable for most plants and has a pH of 6.5–7, acid soils have a lower pH, alkaline ones higher. You can alter the pH by adding lime or peat.

Shredded bark

Mica (large)

Cocoa shells

Coir

Vermiculite

Peat

PEAT AND PEAT SUBSTITUTES
Peat substitutes are made from a number of ingredients. These include coir, cocoa shells, and shredded bark. Vermiculite and mica are added for drainage.

POTTING MIXES

Potting mixes are loam-based, compost-based or peat-based. Loam-based composts all contain some soil. They retain water and nutrients better than peat-based composts and are more suitable for long-term growth. Compost-based mixes contain more nutrients than loam-based mixes and are the best media for established plants and trees.

Peat-based mix (including peat substitutes such as coir) is more readily available, lighter, cleaner and easier to work with. Use it for general gardening in smaller containers.

SPECIAL MIXES

A number of special potting mixes are available, including ericaceous mix for acid-loving plants, orchid mix, alpine and cacti mixes, bulb fibre mix, and hanging basket mix that contains water-retaining granules.

If you live in an area where the soil is very alkaline you can grow acid-loving plants in containers. This applies more to flowers and shrubs than fruit and vegetables, but some fruit, such as blueberries, must be grown in ericaceous soil.

Feeding Container Plants

Container-grown plants need additional feeding to produce good crops. Liquid fertilizer is the easiest to apply, but check which nutrients are most needed.

ABOVE RIGHT *Slow-release granules can be added by hand when growth starts at the beginning of the year.*

All plants need nutrients to survive and grow. In the garden they obtain most of their requirements from the soil but because the area and soil volume in containers is limited and because they are watered more frequently, container-grown plants need regular feeding to thrive and produce the best crops.

FERTILIZER FORMS *Available in organic and non-organic forms. Choose which type you prefer according to your garden.*

BASIC CHEMISTRY

The three main nutrients required by plants are nitrogen (N), phosphorus (P) and potassium (K). Nitrogen is essential for healthy leaf growth, phosphorus for the development of proper root systems and potassium promotes the production of flowers and fruit.

Plants also need a number of trace elements, the most important of which are manganese and magnesium. Nutrients are present in varying proportions in all fertilizers and foliar feeds and are marked on the label. A balanced fertilizer will contain them in equal proportions. This

Inorganic top dressing
These are the easiest to apply. Read the instructions on the packet and check the ratio of the nutrients.

Slow-release granules
Excellent for containers. They release their nutrients over a long period.

Organic fertilizer
Bonemeal, or fish, blood and bone are the most common. Do not use where there are urban rodents.

Slow-release pellets
These are similar to slow-release granules. One application may last a year.

LIQUID FERTILIZERS

1 Mix any liquid fertilizer carefully in a can or spray can that can be kept specially for the purpose. Always follow the maker's instructions on the packet or bottle and do not be tempted to increase the strength of the solution as this may do more harm than good.

2 Foliar feeds are most effective during the summer and should be applied on the "little and often" principle. Plants can be sprayed every two weeks with benefit. It is better to apply any foliar feeds with a small spray can as this is much more economical than applying them with a watering can.

is the best sort to use as a part of your general routine. A high potash (potassium) feed is excellent for tomatoes and fruit when the plants are mature and bearing fruit, but all tender vegetables, such as peppers, require high nitrogen feeds when they are growing to help to establish healthy plants.

NUTRIENT REQUIREMENTS

Permanent plants need fertilizer incorporated in the compost when they are planted. If nutrients are not already present in the compost add bonemeal, a granulated mixture or bonemeal.

Don't use bloodmeal or bonemeal if you live in an area where there are urban rodents because they will dig the plant up time and time again. After planting, all plants should be watered with a weak solution of fertilizer.

GENERAL REQUIREMENTS

Most small herbs will not require feeding other than an application of foliar food if the plants appear spindly or distressed. Vegetable crops, however, need to be fed generously. They require nitrogen-based fertilizers when growth starts in spring followed by potassium-based fertilizer as the plants reach maturity.

Apply fertilizers in liquid form during the growing season, use a liquid fertilizer or foliar feed. Slow-release granules,

however, are invaluable. Add them to the soil at the start of the growing season and one application will serve many plants throughout the year.

USING LIQUID FERTILIZERS

1 Check the nutrients necessary for each plant and take care to apply the correct fertilizer at each stage of the plant's growth. Growing plants need a nitrogen-based fertilizer but you should switch to a potash- (potassium) based fertilizer as the plants reach maturity.

2 Apply the liquid fertilizer to the container and do not water it directly on to the leaves of the plants as this might damage them. Fill the container to the brim and then let the water drain away. Check the instructions to see how often the plants need feeding.

WATERING

1 Watering is essential, especially in summer, and needs to be done every day in hot dry weather. Fill the container to the brim and let the surplus water drain away. Do not just sprinkle the plant and container lightly with water. This will do more harm than good.

2 Be careful when you water any acid-loving plants growing in ericaceous mix if you live in a hard-water area. Either add a small amount of flowers of sulphur to the water or collect rain water in a barrel outside and use that. Check the plants for signs of chlorosis.

Watering Container Plants

Watering is the most important part of container gardening. Without water the plants will die. If you can install an automatic watering system, this solves all problems.

There is absolutely no point in attempting to grow plants in containers, outside, in the summer, unless you are able to water them every day. That is not to say that they have to be watered every day. If it rains all week you certainly won't, but if you go away on holiday for two weeks and this coincides with a hot dry spell don't be surprised if half the garden is dead when you return.

Plants grown in containers need far more moisture than plants grown in the garden. A large container 36 in (90 cm) in diameter may lose up to 1.1 gallons (5 litres) of water each day through the leaves of the plants (transpiration) and evaporation from the container itself, when it is hot and sunny. Terracotta containers are more subject to evaporation than plastic ones but you can overcome this if you line earthenware pots with plastic sheets when they are planted.

TECHNICALITIES

When you water make sure that the container is watered thoroughly. Fill the container to the brim and let this drain

ABOVE *A long-arm attachment for a hose is extremely useful if you have to water a number of hanging baskets.*

Hose
Plastic hoses are available in various lengths. The reinforced ones last longer and are worth the extra expense.

Watering can
Get one with a long arm. It will help you to reach the furthest corners of each container.

down, then repeat. Do not over water. Check the condition of the soil mix rather than the plants. If they show signs of wilting they may be lacking in nutrients or may be waterlogged. If the compost feels dry to the touch more than 1 in (2.5 cm) below the surface then water.

WATERING SYSTEMS

With a large container garden it is well worth installing an automatic watering system. These are computer-controlled and if you have one then all worries about watering vanish. There are three main systems: overhead sprinklers, drip systems, and capillary systems. All have their advantages and disadvantages. Overhead sprinklers are probably the cheapest to install but they use the most water. Drip systems are more expensive but more effective. They deliver water directly to the roots of the plants: there are small drip systems for window boxes and balconies.

Capillary systems, which supply water to the bottom of the plant, are used by nurseries and in greenhouses.

Soaker hose
These can be positioned next to each plant and they will deliver a steady trickle of water to the roots.

TIPS

1 A gravel container filled with water enables the plant to draw up the moisture it needs in a gradual way without the soil mix becoming waterlogged. This is the watering principle adopted in many greenhouses.

2 If a plant appears totally dead and dried out it is worth-while plunging the pot and plant in a bucket of water and leaving it there until the bubbles have stopped rising to the surface. There is a chance that it may recover.

Using Growbags

Growbags are simple. They were traditionally used for growing tomatoes but many other vegetables can be cultivated in them. They make an ideal introduction to container gardening.

ABOVE Outdoor cucumbers are good plants to grow in growbags. Like tomatoes, they can be trained up stakes.

Growbags are a simple way to start off growing vegetables in containers, so the beginner gardener would do well to try out a few plants in them before embarking on a full scale container kitchen garden. They contain a peat-based compost with added nutrients sufficient to establish most plants. Plants grown in growbags will need additional feeding throughout the year.

Traditionally they were used to grow outdoor tomatoes and placed against a warm wall with stakes to which the plants could be trained. However, the range of vegetables that can be cultivated in growbags is much larger. These include, lettuces, peas, bush beans, spinach or Swiss chard. Peas can be allowed to sprawl over the sides of the bag rather than being trained upwards on twigs. This also serves to hide the bags.

USING GROWBAGS

Gardening with growbags is simplicity itself. Put the bag in position and make a number of holes in the base according to the instructions on the side. Cut out the squares on the top of the bag and insert the plants. Three tomato plants fit in a normal bag but if you plan to use one for lettuces or peas, these can be planted quite densely. Plants need to be fed regularly with liquid fertilizer. Aim to cover the whole surface of the growbag when the plants are mature.

GROWBAG PROBLEMS

There are two main problems with growbags. They need to be watered properly every day in summer: modern bags often incorporate a plastic funnel that conveys water along the length. They need also to be concealed for they are not things of any great beauty.

If you have an established patio kitchen garden then you can construct special boxes or troughs into which new bags can be placed each year, or you can have a sunken space on the terrace the right dimensions to take a new bag. This is an excellent idea if you are planning to grow vegetables, such as peas or tomatoes in growbags each year, for it lowers the bag to ground level making it less conspicuous and trailing plants will hide the plastic relatively quickly.

RIGHT Peppers grown outside in a growbag. This patio has purpose-built spaces for growbags that make them less obtrusive.

Overwintering

You need to bring tender plants inside during the winter. If this cannot be done, wrap them up during hard frosts. This also applies to any earthernware containers.

Containers get too hot and dry in summer and conversely they get colder than a surrounding garden in winter because a greater area is exposed to the elements. Plants in containers therefore need special attention in cold winters and may have to be protected, however warm the microclimate of the individual patio, windowsill or roof garden. Roof gardens are particularly affected for being open to the elements they are more likely to be buffeted by wind and storms.

HARDY WINTER VEGETABLES

The container kitchen gardener has less to worry about than the container gardener

growing flowering plants and shrubs. Nearly all vegetables are annuals or grown as annuals and many will have been harvested and removed from the containers before the onset of winter. In the south, any vegetables that remain in containers over winter, such as broccoli, are hardy enough to survive cold and light frost.

PROTECTING HERBS

Herbs are a different matter. Perennial herbs, such as rosemary, thyme and marjoram, all need winter protection. If they cannot be brought inside and kept in a cool, frost-free environment then they can be wrapped in insulating bubble wrap during the hardest months of the year. Heavy row cover material is excellent for it allows light and moisture to penetrate, although it is flimsy and liable to tear if subjected to strong winds and sharp corners. Half-hardy or delicate flowering shrubs also may need protection. Most roses are fully hardy but a few, such as *Rosa banksiae,* are not and should be covered in severe weather.

LOOKING AFTER CONTAINERS

Plants are not the only things that require protection. Terracotta pots may well crumble and crack if they are subjected to extremes of frost and rain. Bind them under the rim with a wire, alternatively wrap them in burlap to guard against

winter frosts. An alternative protection for pots and plants in very hard weather is plastic bubble wrap. Beware: it does not allow the plants to breathe and can contribute to disease.

ABOVE *An outside cover for onions. If they are pulled in wet weather let them dry before storing over the winter.*

BELOW *Tilt containers on their sides and wrap securely with burlap. This gives excellent protection through the winter.*

Pruning, Staking and Supporting

Pruning is quite simple; the main thing is to prune at the correct time of the year and understand the requirements of each plant. Seek advice from a gardening neighbor if in doubt.

ABOVE RIGHT *Large containers can have individual trellises placed at the back to support climbing plants. Wooden containers can have trellises nailed to the back.*

Pruning causes more anxiety than any other gardening activity. However, once you understand the purpose and practice, pruning is perfectly simple. The most important thing to learn is to prune each plant at the correct time of the year.

There are two things to remember: different plants flower and fruit on wood produced in different years, a hybrid tea rose flowers on new wood produced in the current year, peaches flower and fruit on wood produced the previous year; secondly, pruning stimulates growth. The purpose of pruning is to stimulate the correct growth to produce the optimum amount of flowers and fruit.

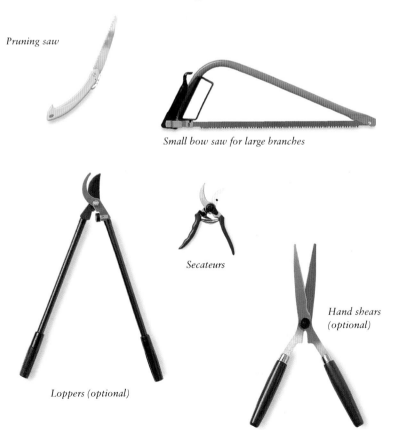

Pruning saw

Small bow saw for large branches

Secateurs

Hand shears (optional)

Loppers (optional)

CORRECT PRUNING

Young plants can be pruned when first planted to a few strong shoots. Leave two buds on each pruned shoot and new growth will spring from them in the right direction the following year. Roses and currant bushes are both pruned in this way when they are first planted. Make sure that your secateurs are sharp and that the cuts are clean with no ragged edges for this can contribute to disease. Bypass secateurs are the best as the straight-edged secateurs tend to crush the branches when making the cut. Detailed pruning instructions are given opposite and on page 144.

Most herbs and small shrubs have few specific pruning requirements other than keeping them tidy and in shape. Trees, on the other hand, need to be trained and supported, and those in large containers may need to be secured firmly in position, especially on an exposed roof garden subject to high winds.

PRUNING IN THE CONTAINER GARDEN

Climbing roses: The best climbing roses for a relatively restricted space are climbers with hybrid tea-shaped flowers or the climbing varieties of hybrid tea and floribunda roses.

At planting, trim any damaged roots, train the shoots and prune back any damaged growth; cut out any weak side shoots. The following summer tie in the side shoots as growth develops, and train the shoots into a fan. Deadhead the rose after flowering. Early the following year cut back all the flowering laterals (side shoots) to 3–4 eyes or 6 in (15 cm) and tie in any shoots to form a framework. Repeat this on an annual basis, removing main branches after a year or two if they show signs of exhaustion to within 2 in (5 cm) of the ground. This stimulates new growth from the base.

CLIMBING PLANTS

Jasmine: Summer jasmine is a vigorous plant and may need cutting back to keep within bounds. After flowering thin any old weak wood and cut out up to one-third of the shoots if necessary. Tie in new growths as they develop.

Winter jasmine: Prune after flowering in early spring. Cut back all the shoots that have flowered by one third. Cut out completely any shoots that appear weak or damaged.

Hop: A vigorous climber. Cut back hard in the spring to within 2–3 ft (60–90 cm) of the ground to keep it within bounds.

BELOW *Almost all plants benefit from staking. Push the stake in down the side of the container.*

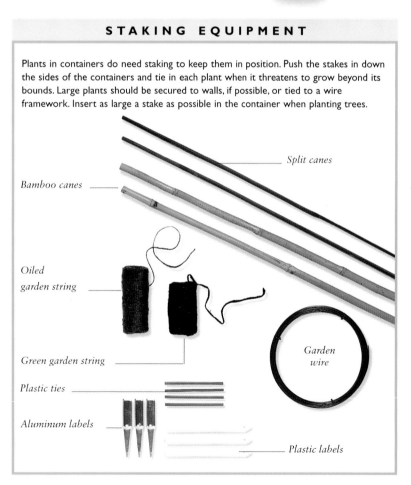

STAKING EQUIPMENT

Plants in containers do need staking to keep them in position. Push the stakes in down the sides of the containers and tie in each plant when it threatens to grow beyond its bounds. Large plants should be secured to walls, if possible, or tied to a wire framework. Insert as large a stake as possible in the container when planting trees.

Split canes

Bamboo canes

Oiled garden string

Green garden string

Garden wire

Plastic ties

Aluminum labels

Plastic labels

Pruning, Staking and Supporting

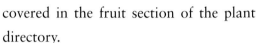

RIGHT Newly planted trees need to be secured to a stake with proper tree ties to avoid chafing the bark.

HERBS AND SHRUBS

Trim all shrubby herbs, such as thyme, sage and marjoram, to keep them neat in their container in early spring. Apart from this they do not need specific pruning. *Rosemary*: Cut back any misplaced shoots in the spring but beware, rosemary will not regenerate if it is cut back into the hard wood.

Lavender: Prune lavender hard each mid spring to stimulate new growth. Cut all flowering shoots right back to within 1 in (2.5 cm) of last year's wood.

FRUIT TREES AND CURRANTS

The pruning of pears, apples, figs and peaches is covered in the fruit section of the plant directory.

Apples and pears are normally trained as cordons or espaliers (see page 144). Pruning figs is quite complicated and you need to consult a specialist pruning manual. Quinces and medlars have few specific pruning requirements

---

TRELLIS SUPPORTS

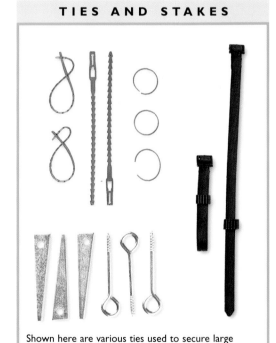

Trellis is available at all garden centers. Measure the amount you need and check that it is properly made. If you are erecting a trellis in a confined space you may have to construct your own to ensure that it fits accurately and neatly.

Secure it to the walls with molly bolts leaving a good 1½ in (3.75 cm) gap for the air to circulate. Never intertwine plants such as roses through a trellis. Always train in the branches by tying them to the front with garden twine.

TIES AND STAKES

Shown here are various ties used to secure large branches and trees to stakes. It is important not to chafe branches as this may cause disease. Vine eyes and bolts are essential for securing wire properly to walls. Vine eyes can be hammered directly in but bolts need molly wings to secure them properly.

apart from the removal of weak and crossing branches.

Plums: These need little pruning once the basic shape has been established. Prune in the summer not winter or early spring.

Cherries and Morello cherries: To train a cherry tree as a fan against a wall follow the steps outlined for training peach trees on page 144. Pruning a mature fan is very similar to pruning a peach. It may be necessary to cut back some of the older side shoots each spring to within 3–4 in (7.5–10 cm) of their base to stimulate the basal buds to produce new growth.

Currants: See the plant directory.

SUPPORTING

Containers may blow over in high winds, especially if they are on an exposed roof garden and are top-heavy with trees or shrubs. It is most important to ensure that all containers are supported securely and it may be necessary to secure them with guy ropes or wire fastened to ring bolts on the roof or walls of the garden.

STAKING

Check that all plants are thoroughly secure. Small climbing plants can be trained up custom-built trellises that can be inserted into the containers themselves or up trellises attached to walls. You may, if you wish, attach a trellis directly to the back of any wooden container screwing it in place.

All trees and shrubs will need a supporting stake in place when they are first planted and you can surround tall-growing plants with bamboo canes in order to enclose them and keep them upright. All large trees require staking at planting.

GROWING PEAS IN A POT

1 Choose a good-sized earthenware pot and put adequate drainage in the bottom. Fill with potting compost, leaving a 1 in (2.5 cm) gap at the top.

2 Remove each plant from the growing pot and firm it into the potting soil around the edge of the container. Leave a 4 in (10 cm) space between each.

3 Add stakes between the plants. Pea sticks cut from hedges were traditionally used in the country for growing peas. They also helped to deter birds.

4 Make sure that the roots of each plant are undisturbed when you insert the supporting canes. Tie these loosely together if necessary.

Propagation – *sowing seeds and planting out*

Sowing seeds is the first step to growing your own produce. Check the seed packet for details and follow the instructions. Handle young seedlings carefully.

ABOVE RIGHT
A proper propagating frame with humidity and temperature controls is a great help when sowing seeds or taking cuttings.

Sowing seeds is the easiest way to propagate plants. In a container garden only sow seeds in position (*in situ*) if the plants will be difficult to prick out and transplant: carrots and beets for example. Other vegetables can be sown in a tray of seedling mix, pricked out and transplanted when they are mature enough.

PRACTICAL INSTRUCTIONS FOR SOWING

If you are sowing seeds in seed trays ensure that there is proper drainage in the bottom and then fill the tray with seedling mix, water the mix and allow it to drain. Sow seeds according to directions on the packet. If sowing seeds *in situ*, choose the site in your container where you want the seeds to grow. Rake and prepare the medium and sow a few seeds in each position. If you are sowing large seeds, such as peas or beans, sow roughly double the number you need and remove the weakest plants if they all germinate. When sowing fine seeds, such as carrots or chives, scatter the seed thinly and thin the plants when they germinate.

ABOVE *Small seeds can be sown in disposable individual cardboard cells or peat pots. Sow two seeds and discard one if both germinate.*

SOWING FINE SEEDS

1 Fill the tray with a good seed starter mix. Firm the mix to within ½ in (1.25 cm) of the top. Scatter fine and medium-sized seeds evenly on the surface.

2 If the seed needs dark conditions to germinate, use a fine screen to cover the seed with the required amount of mix. Do not cover the seed too deeply.

3 Stand the tray in a shallow bowl of water until the mix surface moistens. Leave to drain. Cover the tray with a sheet of plastic wrap and place it somewhere warm.

PRICKING OUT AND TRANSPLANTING

If you have sown a number of seeds, you will need to prick out the seedlings when they appear. Wait until they have two pairs of leaves and then gently lever the small plants from the seed container and replant them in multi-purpose potting soil. Hold the seedlings by the seed leaves, the bottom ones, and not by the stem. Replant to the same depth as before and firm the mix gently around the small plant. Harden seedlings off and transplant in position when the plants are large enough.

TEMPERATURE

All seeds have a minimum temperature that has to be reached before they will germinate and this varies from plant to plant. The seed packet will carry this information. Generally, seeds of ordinary vegetables will not germinate until the soil temperature has been above 45°F (7°C) for a week.

CARE OF SEEDLINGS

Seedlings are sometimes subject to "damping-off," a fungal disease that usually occurs when seedlings are too crowded or the compost is cold and too wet. Spray the seedlings from time to time with a suitable fungicide as an avoidance measure and take care to keep all containers as clean as possible.

If you have trays on a windowsill turn the tray every day as otherwise the plants will grow lopsided towards the light. Put them outside as soon as possible, and shade them from direct sunlight to start with. If you leave young plants in seedling mix for some time they will need feeding with a diluted liquid fertilizer.

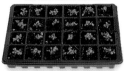

ABOVE Once seedlings are large enough to handle, transfer them individually to a tray of growing medium, allowing 1½–2 in (4–5 cm) around each one.

SOWING LARGE SEEDS

1 For easier handling, sow large seeds in a container. Fill the pot with seed starter mix and level off the top.

2 To insure that there are no air pockets in the soil, gently firm and level the mix with a flat-bottomed utensil, like a glass.

3 Making sure there is a space between the top of the mix and the pot rim, spot sow the seeds evenly on the surface.

4 Cover the seed with a layer of mix if it needs darkness to germinate. Water the pot from below. Cover it with plastic wrap.

Propagation – *taking cuttings and division*

Growing plants from cuttings or increasing the number of plants by division is one of the most satisfying things in all gardening. There is no mystery about it, it is really very easy.

ABOVE RIGHT *Mint is an invasive plant that spreads by its surface roots. Cut these up and replant to increase your stock.*

There are many diffent types of cuttings but the principle is the same for all. Cut off a shoot, dip it in hormone rooting powder, and replant it in moist peat-based mix. Keep the cuttings moist, preferably in a propagating frame.

SEMI-RIPE CUTTINGS

These are taken in late summer from new wood of the current year. Choose a non-flowering shoot. Cuttings 2–4 in (5–10 cm) long are about the normal length. Trim them just below a leaf joint

TAKING SEMI-RIPE CUTTINGS

1 Cut off some shoots in summer (rosemary is shown here). Shoots without flowers make the best cuttings.

2 Separate out all the shoots and then strip off the lower leaves, leaving a stem to be inserted into rooting medium.

3 Mist the cuttings with water before you insert them in the mix. Cuttings need a moist atmosphere.

4 Prepare a potting mix with plenty of sand to improve the drainage. Insert the cuttings round the edge of the pot.

5 Put a wire loop over the pot. An old coat hanger can be cut up for this. Pull a large plastic bag over the loop.

6 Make sure the compost is moist and then secure the bag with a large elastic band around the rim of the pot.

7 Rooted cuttings in the same container that have doubled in size. They can now be planted in individual pots.

8 Pot up each cutting in good potting soil with drainage in each container. Feed them with liquid fertilizer.

and remove the lower leaves. If necessary remove some leaves to reduce moisture-loss. Dip the cutting in rooting powder and insert in the cutting medium.

Some shrubs and herbs root best from semi-ripe cuttings taken with a heel of the old wood. Pull the shoot away from the plant in a downwards direction and it will come away with a heel of wood. Trim this if necessary.

HARDWOOD CUTTINGS

These are taken in the fall from new shoots that have completed their first year of growth. Cut up into lengths 10–12 in (25–30 cm) long. Trim at the top to above a pair of buds and at the bottom to below a pair of buds. Remove a sliver of wood from the base. Insert them in a trench with coarse sand or peerlite in the bottom to aid drainage, 3–4 in (7.5–10 cm) apart, to at least half

their depth. They may take a long time to grow roots. Leave them undisturbed for a year unless they have obviously failed.

DIVISION

This is the simplest form of propagation and is explained above.

ROOT DIVISION

Dig up any suitable plant, one that spreads by forming new roots, either in the spring or after flowering, whichever is more appropriate. Pull the plant apart either by hand, with the help of two garden forks or divide up the rootball with a knife. Then replant the divisions right away: a good example of a plant that can be increased by division is the primrose.

ABOVE *Some plants will root happily in jars of water without any requirement to put them in soil. Keep cuttings on a windowsill and when the roots are fully formed they can be potted up individually.*

PROPAGATING GARLIC

1 Garlic is easy to propagate using cloves broken from a bulb. Either plant these directly into the soil or put them in a plastic bag where they will sprout before they are planted out.

2 Close the bag and leave them until they start to form shoots. You will be able to see these. Plant them out 2 in (5 cm) deep in spring and they can be lifted at the end of the summer.

ROOTING HORMONE

Many semi-ripe cuttings, such as pelargoniums, root better if they are dipped in hormone rooting powder before putting them into the potting compost.

Maintaining and Cleaning Containers

Looking after your containers is very important. They need to be kept clean and well drained. Support them on blocks to allow the air to circulate underneath and this will prolong their life.

ABOVE RIGHT *Wooden barrels need to be soaked in water to close up the staves before use. Plunge them in water overnight.*

All containers must be suitable for their purpose. They must fit the plant and they must contain sufficient soil mix for that plant to flourish. They must be strong enough to withstand the elements. They must also have adequate drainage to allow surplus water to drain away when the plants are watered.

DRAINAGE

Almost all garden containers that you can purchase will have proper drainage holes already in place but if they don't you will have to make holes in the bottom. The same thing applies if you have made the containers yourself. Make sure that there are enough drainage holes and if you are lining the container with polyethene see that there are holes in the polyethene that align with the holes in the bottom of the container.

THE CORRECT HARDCORE

Prepared containers must include sufficient gravel, crocks, broken pottery or small stones, in the bottom to keep the

CLEANING A USED POT

1 Remove any old growing medium and plant debris by scrubbing the pot, inside and out, with a wire brush or stiff household brush.

2 Wash the container thoroughly with detergent and warm water, then rinse well with clean water before refilling with fresh growing medium.

mix aerated and ensure that it does not run out of the drainage holes when the container is watered.

Make sure that any drainage material used in the bottom of a pot of ericaceous mix does not contain any lime. For example, limestone chippings and old mortar are obvious sources of lime and should be avoided.

CLEANING

Containers should be cleaned after use to prevent the spread of disease. Scrub them thoroughly to remove all dirt and if necessary soak them overnight in soapy water. Ensure that they are completely dry before filling and re-using.

WOODEN CONTAINERS

These need to be treated with a preservative recommended for horticultural use before they are first planted. Make sure that you use one that is safe for plants and follow the instructions on the label. Preservatives such as creosote should be avoided at all costs because they kill plants.

You can also extend the life of a wooden container by lining it with plastic. Make holes in the bottom of the plastic for drainage and then fix it to the sides of the container with a staple gun.

It is also a good idea to line the sides of any copper, iron or lead containers that you are using in order to prevent the metallic elements of the container leaching into the mix which might affect the plants.

ALLOW AIR TO CIRCULATE

Also raise all containers off the ground slightly, in order to promote drainage and allow air to circulate, by putting them on wooden blocks or special clay feet. This is a particularly important consideration for wooden containers because if they are allowed to sit permanently in damp they will gradually rot.

MOVING CONTAINERS

Large containers full of plants can be heavy and difficult to move. There are a number of ways to do this. You can try and manoeuvre the container onto a piece of burlap and then pull the burlap to where you want it to be. You can put it on a board and then put small rollers under the board in the same way as boats used to be launched, or you can make a rope cradle round the container, attach the ends to a strong pole and lift it with the help of a couple of strong men. In all these cases you may want to wrap up the plants to protect them while they are being moved.

One way of moving a container is to put it on a board and use sections of pipe as rollers.

Pests and Diseases

Prevention is better than cure so the best thing is a healthy environment for all plants. Examine them daily and take action immediately if diseases or pests appear.

ABOVE RIGHT *Earwig traps can be used for any infested plants. Put flower pots upside down on canes and fill them with straw. Each day empty them and burn the straw. The earwigs shelter in the straw and only emerge as dusk falls.*

All plants suffer pests and diseases. Prevention is much better than cure and all gardeners should try and create a healthy environment for their plants.

THE IMPORTANCE OF VENTILATION

As a first rule, try to ensure adequate air circulation (although this may be difficult to achieve if you are growing a large number of plants in a small place such as a balcony or patio). On fruit trees and shrubs, pay particular attention to pruning and ensure that the center of each plant is open so that air can circulate.

CONTROLLING PESTS

Your approach to spraying and pest control will depend on how strictly you adhere to organic principles. There are organic alternatives to most garden pesticides, but they may not be as effective as non-organic brands. It is important that

COMMON PESTS

Aphids
The best-known aphids are greenfly and blackfly. They all suck the sap from the plant and weaken it.
Control: Pinch out the growing tip of any broad beans infected by blackfly. Spray with a contact or systemic insecticide or a solution of insecticidal soap. This is often effective.

Leaf miners
Small insect larvae that feed inside the leaves of the plant. Eventually the whole leaf may be destroyed.
Control: Pick off infected leaves or spray with a pesticide as soon as the damage appears. Spraying may have to be repeated every two weeks in cases of bad infestation.

Red spider mites
Tiny orange-red or yellowish mites with black markings. They suck the sap of plants and cause considerable damage in a greenhouse.
Control: Keep the atmosphere moist or spray with a suitable pesticide. The biological control *Phytoseiulus persimilis* can be effective.

Black vine weevil larvae
A major pest that can cause plants to wilt, collapse and disintegrate. Examine the roots of the plant for the white grubs.
Control: The parasitic nematode *Heterorhabditis megidis*, is the best control for any container plant affected. Otherwise dust the soil mix with pesticide powder in summer.

you always read the instructions on the labels carefully.

COMPANION PLANTING

Some plants deter unwelcome insects. For example, French marigolds and tomatoes deter imported cabbage moths from laying their eggs on brassicas when planted close by. Mint and some strong smelling herbs have the same effect. With careful planting, caterpillars can be a thing of the past.

OTHER COMMON PESTS

Ants: These common pests feed on the honeydew excreted by aphids and carry them from plant to plant. They damage the roots of plants by tunnelling and eat newly sown seeds. Destroy nests with boiling water; dust areas with a recommended insecticide or apply a residual product that forms a lasting barrier.

Birds: Troublesome when it comes to fruit or brassicas, birds are unlikely to cause as much damage as they do in a large traditional kitchen garden. Scarecrows are fairly ineffective. The only solution is to net everything at risk.

Carrot fly: The larvae of the carrot fly tunnel into the roots of the vegetables. Deter by enclosing the carrots with a barrier; the flies do not fly far off the ground – 2 ft (60 cm) is usually sufficient.

DIAGNOSING TROUBLE

If your plants are invaded by pests these can usually be recognized. Diseases and deficiencies are more difficult as many have the same symptoms. Before jumping to the conclusion that you have fire blight or downy mildew, test your soil mix with a soil testing kit. If it hasn't been renewed it may well be lacking in one of the nutrients, nitrogen, phosphate or potassium which can be added in fertilizers.

Earwigs
These may do a considerable amount of damage to young vegetables, eating away the leaves.
Control: Put straw inside upturned pots and put them on stakes among the plants. Earwigs hide there in the day when they can be killed. Spray with pesticide spray at dusk.

Scale insects
Another sap-sucking pest usually found on fruit bushes or in the greenhouse. Some excrete honeydew which leads to sooty mold.
Control: Use the parasitic wasp *Metaphycus helvolus* as a biological control. Spray with a suitable pesticide, but several applications may be necessary. These work best on nymphs.

Slugs and snails
These can be a major problem. Young brassicas and lettuces are prone to slug damage.
Control: Trap them under an (eaten) upturned grapefruit half, or by sinking a shallow pot half-filled with sweet liquid in the soil mix. Deter them with collars of plastic or sharp sand around the plants. Use slug pellets sparingly.

Wireworms
Small yellow grubs that feed on the roots of many plants. The leaves turn yellow and wilt. Young seedlings usually die if attacked.
Control: Use a soil insecticide available in granular form, work it into the top 1 in (2.5 cm) of soil. They are not normally troublesome in containers.

Pests and Diseases

Caterpillars: Companion planting will go a long way to avoiding these. If your vegetables do become infected with caterpillars, pick then off by hand and spray with a suitable pesticide.

Nematodes: These cause serious damage and there is no control readily available for the amateur gardener. However, they are unlikely to affect any plants grown in containers for they are generally soil borne.

Sawfly: These cause serious damage to fruit especially gooseberries. Apples, pears and cherries can also be affected.

Spray with a suitable insecticide.

Slugs and earwigs: Can be trapped or picked off by hand.

Squirrels: Birds may be bad but squirrels are far worse. If you are affected there are two ways to deal with them. One is to erect a permanent wire barrier over everything; netting simply isn't strong enough to keep them out. The other is a squirrel trap.

Whitefly: The nymph of these small creatures attacks brassicas out of doors and they are also common pests of the

RIGHT *Insufficient green pigment in the leaves (chlorosis) may be due to excess lime in the soil.*

COMMON DISEASES

Gray mold (botrytis)
This is caused by damp conditions and affects fruit such as strawberries. There is little that can be done to arrest the disease, but keeping the plants dry and as well-ventilated as possible and removing any infected fruit and leaves will help to prevent it.
Control: Botrytis can be treated with fungicide but it is better to avoid creating the conditions in which it occurs although this may be difficult if the summer is cold and damp.

Downy mildew
This is caused by various species of fungi. Young seedlings can be particularly prone and most young plants die. It shows as white mealy growth on the underside of the foliage and the upper surface may become blotched or discolored.
Control: The disease may be prevented by watering young plants so that the roots are moist. Improved ventilation helps and also avoid any overcrowding. Spray with the fungicide, mancozeb.

Fire blight
This is a serious disease that is confined to the Rosaceae family. If the disease does break out the plant will look scorched and dark. Greenish brown cankers form on the branches. Luckily it is relatively rare.
Control: There is only one thing to do if the plant is affected by fire blight and that is to dig up and remove the plant right away. Do not plant any other members of the rose family in the same place for at least three years.

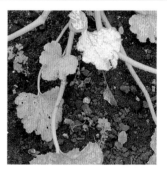

Powdery mildew
This is different from downy mildew and shows as a white powdery coating on the leaves and stems of the plant. It is quite common on roses, peas and gooseberries and some other vegetables. Affected leaves may drop.
Control: Spray with a suitable fungicide during the summer, pick off and dispose of any affected leaves and shoots. Keep all plants well mulched and watered in the growing season.

greenhouse. Spray with a suitable insecticide and repeat as necessary.

OTHER COMMON DISEASES

Black spot: Common on roses. Spray regularly with a suitable fungicide.

Canker: Shrunken scars that appear on the shoots of woody plants, especially apple, pear and plum trees in summer. Cut off the infected branches right away and dispose of them; paint the wound with fungicide paint.

Fungal diseases: These cause mold, mildew and wilt and thrive in humid conditions. All fungal disease is difficult to control. High air circulation is the best way to prevent them. The same applies to leaf spot but in this case a fungicidal spray may prove effective, particularly on young leaves.

Scab: This affects fruit and potatoes and first shows as black spots on young leaves. Spray with suitable fungicide.

PLANT DISORDERS

As well as pests and diseases, plants suffer from a number of common disorders. These include frost and prolonged drought. Leave all frost damaged plants until well into the summer before digging up and throwing away. Water in periods of drought. Other disorders are most likely to be caused by nutrient or trace element deficiencies in the soil. Test for nitrogen, potassium and phosphate and add when necessary.

Coral spot
The container gardener is unlikely to be affected by coral spot as this disease usually only attacks old wood although there are cases where it moves from a dead branch to a live one. Fruit trees such as apples and gooseberries may sometimes be affected.
Control: Cut out any affected wood in summer when you see it. Cut back into healthy wood and immediately remove all prunings from the base of the plant.

Silver leaf
This is a serious disease that affects plums and cherries. It first shows as a silvery sheen on the leaves and the plants wither and die with fungus growths appearing on the dead wood.
Control: The disease is really only active in the winter so all prunus varieties should be pruned in the summer. When a tree is affected cut it right back into good wood but if the disease has a strong hold the plant will have to be dug up and disposed of.

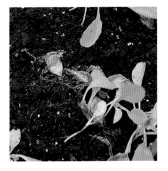

Damping off
A disease of seedlings which makes them collapse and die. It is usually caused by damp soil that is too cold or overcrowding. If it is left a fluffy white fungal growth will appear on the seed trays.
Control: Water seedlings regularly with a suitable fungicide, throw away any trays of seedlings that are affected and disinfect the seed trays. Use sterilized seedling mix and seed that has been pretreated with the appropriate fungicide.

Mosaic virus
There are a number of viruses that may affect different plants but they all have the same symptoms. The virus is an organism that lives inside the plant and feeds on it. Leaves turn yellow and growth is distorted with poor misshapen fruit. Tomatoes and raspberries are particularly affected.
Control: Buy certified virus-free stock. Control aphids rigorously. Dig up and throw away any affected plants right away and rotate vegetable crops.

Harvesting and Storing

Ripe vegetables and fruit wait for no one. Always harvest your crops when they are ready and if they cannot be eaten right away, dry them or freeze them for use later.

ABOVE *Always harvest young vegetables when they are fresh; many become overripe quickly. Freeze any surplus that you cannot use immediately.*

TOP RIGHT *Many vegetables can be dried and hung up until you wish to use them. Onions are the best-known example. Treat chillies the same way.*

It is unlikely that the harvest from your container kitchen garden will be large enough to cause any major storage problems. However, that said, there is every reason to do what you can to ensure that nothing is wasted and that you are able to make the most of your harvest and enjoy all the fruit, vegetables and herbs that you have grown when you want to eat them.

PLANNING TO AVOID A GLUT

Take care when planning your garden not to grow too many of one type of vegetable that will ripen all at the same time. Do not overestimate your requirements.

Try to time your planting to produce a staggered harvest. For example, in the summer you may only wish to eat a lettuce every other day, seven in two weeks. Don't therefore plant a dozen F1 hybrids that will mature at the same time, instead plant six and another six two weeks later.

DRYING AND STORING

If you have sufficient space, a number of vegetables, such as onions and potatoes, can be dried and stored in a cool dry, dark place for several weeks. Carrots and beets can also be stored in wooden boxes of sand.

Most other vegetables can be frozen. They usually need blanching first, so plunge them into boiling water for a few minutes, drain and then freeze them. Follow directions in a cookbook for precise instructions on how to freeze each vegetable.

FRUIT

As much fruit as possible should be eaten when it is ripe even if you have to have a large dinner party in order to do so. This particularly applies to strawberries that are very unsatisfactory when frozen, although they can be pulped, frozen and then used as a purée at a pinch.

Apples can be stored in a cool dry place provided they are absolutely free from all blemishes. Some varieties keep better than others; generally the later varieties will keep, the early ones, such as 'Discovery', won't. Pears, too, can be kept for a time wrapped in paper in a cool dark place.

Most other fruit, all the currants, berries, even plums, freeze perfectly well and the kitchen container gardener should take the trouble to do this. Frozen fruit can bring a welcome taste of late summer into a winter's day. It is very satisfying to eat your own poached plums, or gooseberry crumble, on a dark day in midwinter when all thoughts of summer have passed.

The easiest method of freezing most fruit is to freeze them individually on trays and then put the frozen fruit in bags. Larger fruit, such as plums, should be rinsed in clean water first, smaller berries and currants should be frozen dry as they are picked. Remember to top and tail currants and gooseberries before freezing.

HERBS

Many herbs can be dried, and this was the traditional way of preserving them. The most practical way to dry herbs is to pick them and lay them on paper on a table in an airy room, turning them over once a day; the roots of a number of herbs, particularly medicinal ones, can be dug up and dried.

A number of herbs that do not dry well can be frozen. These include basil, tarragon, fennel, chervil, parsley and chives. Store them in plastic bags.

BELOW Carrots and beets can be covered with dry sand and used throughout the winter.

the
Plant
directory

The plants in this directory are divided into three groups; herbs, vegetables and fruit. Within each group, plants are listed alphabetically under their Latin name. Each entry gives a description of the plant and growing advice. Plants are categorized as tender, half-hardy, frost-hardy or hardy. These groupings are only a guide. In temperate climates, severe frost before midwinter may do little damage to plants; in early spring it may kill them.

TENDER Tolerates temperatures down to 41°F (5°C)

HALF-HARDY Down to 32°F (0°C)

FROST-HARDY Down to 23°F (−5°C)

HARDY Down to 5°F (−15°C)

LEFT *An antique pot of herbs essential for the cook and placed nearby on the patio. The varying leaf shapes and colors of the mints, sage, parsley and chives make a pleasing contrast, like a flower arrangement.*

Herbs

Herbs in containers should be positioned close to the kitchen so they can easily be picked. Most are easy to grow and even a small container or trough will produce enough for everyday use in the kitchen.

Container herbs can be planned in three ways; small containers can be devoted to individual herbs – this is very satisfactory for plants such as mint that are very invasive; a large container can be divided up into compartments in imitation of the traditional herb garden; or a number of herbs can be planted together in one container, grouped for color and contrast. Fresh herbs add a delicious flavor to dishes and are generally sweeter and stronger than dried ones.

CAUTION A number of herbs possess healing properties but they must not be eaten or applied in their raw state in the home. For example the medicinal garden plant, the common foxglove, Digitalis purpurea, is used to treat heart disease in conventional and homeopathic medicine but is extremely poisonous in its raw state.

(NOTE Soil preferences are given for plants in open ground. This provides an indication of the type and richness of the most suitable soil mix and growing conditions when grown in a container.)

Achillea millefolium
Yarrow

Yarrow is a decorative perennial herb that can be planted in containers to add color and form to a herbal arrangement. It was formerly used in folk medicine to staunch wounds and also as a digestive tonic and dye plant. The young leaves can be used sparingly in salads or dried and smoked as a herbal tobacco. Yarrow needs controlling, for it is invasive and is usually grown in herbaceous borders. There are a number of cultivars with flowers of differing colors from white to deep red and yellow. The flowerheads can be cut and dried and are useful in dried flower arrangements.

HARDY (Zone 3).
HEIGHT 6–24 in (15–60 cm).
FLOWERS White, pink or red depending on the cultivar, borne in flat clusters at the end of the flower stalk.
FLOWERING Midsummer to fall.
FOLIAGE Lance shaped with many divided leaves that give the plant a lacy appearance; hence *millefolium*, literally "a thousand leaves."
SOIL Poor, well drained. Good for alkaline soils and seaside gardens.
SITE Sun or partial shade.
PROPAGATION By seed sown in the spring or divide in spring or fall.
USES Medicinal, culinary, dried flowers.
OTHER VARIETIES AND SPECIES
A. millefolium 'Cerise Queen', *A. m.* 'Sammetriese', *A. ptarmica* (Sneezewort).

Adonis vernalis
Spring Adonis

The legend has it that this attractive yellow spring-flowering perennial sprang from the blood of Adonis, lover of Venus, when he was killed by a boar. It is used as a heart tonic and the flowers are a brilliant sight when they open in the spring, turning to catch the sun's rays. The plant will grow in containers in full sun or partial shade and likes well drained, fertile soil with the addition of some leaf mold.

HARDY (Zone 5).
HEIGHT AND SPREAD 8 in (20 cm).
FLOWERS Golden-yellow, star-shaped on short stems with up to 20 petals.
FLOWERING Early spring.
FOLIAGE Light green, finely divided and feathery.
SOIL Well drained alkaline loam.
SITE Sun or partial shade.
PROPAGATION Sow seeds *in situ* in fall, divide after flowering.
USES Medicinal
OTHER VARIETIES AND SPECIES
A. aestivalis, *A. amurensis*, *A. a.* 'Flore Pleno', *A. annua*.

RIGHT *The yellow flowers and delicate foliage of Spring Adonis bring a cheerful touch to containers early in the year.*

Agastache foeniculum
Anise Hyssop

This perennial native herb from the prairies of North America carries long spikes of violet-blue flowers from midsummer to early fall. The flowers are attractive to bees. The leaves are anise-scented, hence the common name. A tea made from the leaves is used in herbal medicine for coughs and colds and the leaves can also be used for flavoring. The dried flowers are a good ingredient in pot pourri.

HARDY (Zone 5).
HEIGHT AND SPREAD 3–5 ft (90–150 cm) by 12 in (30 cm).
FLOWERS Purple-blue held in long spikes.
FLOWERING Late summer to fall.
FOLIAGE Triangular, sharply toothed leaves on short stalks. The leaves are aromatic.
SOIL Well drained loam.
SITE Full sun.
PROPAGATION Sow seed in spring at 55–64°F (13–18°C). Divide in spring or take semi-ripe cuttings in late summer. Keep frost-free in winter.
USES Medicinal, culinary, bee plant.
OTHER VARIETIES AND SPECIES
A. barberi, *A. foeniculum* 'Alabaster', (white flowers), *A. mexicana*.

Allium sativum
Garlic

Common garlic can be classed either as a herb or a vegetable. It is a close relation of the onion, and its growth habit and appearance are similar. Garlic is probably the most commonly used herb in the kitchen. Many famous dishes are based on garlic, such as *aïoli*, a garlicky mayonnaise dip from Provence. Garlic is also much valued in herbal medicine, as a digestive and in the treatment of high blood pressure. It is also supposed to ward off the common cold.

HARDY (Zone 3).
HEIGHT 6–12 in (30–60 cm).
FLOWERS Each plant has a single head of pale pink or greenish-white flowers with a number of bulbils.
FLOWERING Summer.
FOLIAGE Short, flat, upright gray-green leaves.
SOIL Well drained, light, alkaline soil.
SITE Open and sunny.
PROPAGATION Plant individual cloves in the fall approximately 4 in (10 cm) deep and 7 in (18 cm) apart. Most varieties need at least two months at temperatures between 32–50°F (0–10°C). Do not plant on ground that has been recently manured.
USES Culinary, medicinal.
OTHER VARIETIES AND SPECIES
A. cernuum (wild onion), *A. ursinum* (wild garlic), *A. vineale* (crow garlic).

Allium schoenoprasum
Chives

Chives are perennial bulbs that can be grown as a decorative edging in containers or borders. They prefer fertile soil that does not dry out. Both flowers and leaves are used in the kitchen as a flavoring and a garnish; the flowers make an attractive edible decoration for salads. Surplus leaves can be frozen for use during the winter, when the foliage dies down completely. If you are growing chives for culinary use rather than decoration, cut the plant to the ground two or three times during the growing season to promote fresh growth.

HARDY (Zone 3).
HEIGHT 8–12 in (20–30 cm).
FLOWERS Pink or purple many-petalled flowers on long stalks.
FLOWERING Summer.
FOLIAGE Long thin green leaves.
SOIL Prefers moist rich loam.
SITE Open and sunny.
PROPAGATION Sow in seed trays indoors in spring and then plant out in groups of three or four seedlings. Established groups can be divided every three or four years in spring or fall.
USES Culinary.
OTHER VARIETIES AND SPECIES
A. schoenoprasum var. *sibiricum* (Siberian chives), *A. s.* 'Forescate' (pink flowers).

RIGHT *The light purple flowers of chives,* Allium Schoenoprasum, *are delightful in summer. They are sometimes grown to edge a large container.*

Aloysia triphylla
Lemon Verbena

This deciduous shrub requires protection during the winter in temperate climates. The leaves are highly aromatic and the essential oil (Spanish verbena) distilled from them can be used as flavoring in cakes, drinks and in pot pourris. Tea made from the leaves, sold in France as vervaine, is soothing in cases of indigestion.

CAUTION Large doses or prolonged use can cause internal irritation.

HALF-HARDY (Zones 7–10).
HEIGHT 6 ft (1.8 m) or more in its natural habitat.
FLOWERS Pale lilac to white held on slender clustered spikes.
FLOWERING Late summer.
FOLIAGE Narrow, lance-shaped, bright green leaves that have oil-bearing glands on the underside.
SOIL Rich, well drained.
SITE Full sun.
PROPAGATION Take semi-ripe cuttings in summer and root under mist (keep the leaves moist).
USES Culinary, medicinal.
OTHER VARIETIES AND SPECIES None.

Anethum graveolens
Dill

Dill is an attractive plant, with its fine feathery leaves and flat yellow flowerheads made up of a multitude of small bright yellow flowers. It is a popular herb in the kitchen, especially in the Scandinavian countries where it is used in pickling and fish dishes, most famously in *gravadlax*, salmon pickled with dill. The flowers can also be cut and dried for flower arranging. The main parts used in the kitchen are the leaves, which should be picked when young and fresh (they can be frozen for use later), and the seeds. These are more strongly flavored than the leaves and are used in baking.

HARDY ANNUAL.
HEIGHT 2–3 ft (60–90 cm).
FLOWERS Small yellow held on flat heads.
FLOWERING Summer.
FOLIAGE Blue-green fine, feathery leaves.
SOIL Prefers dry conditions.
SITE Full sun.
PROPAGATION Sow seed in spring where the plants are to grow. Thin to 12 in (30 cm) apart.
USES Culinary, dried flowers.
OTHER VARIETIES AND SPECIES
A. graveolens 'Dukat', *A. g.* 'Sowa'.

Anthriscus cerefolium
Chervil

Chervil is a fine and delicate herb, both in appearance and flavor. It has fern-like leaves, small white flowers and a flavor reminiscent of aniseed. It is used to flavor soups and stews and should be added at the last minute otherwise the flavor will be lost in cooking. It grows best in shade and is a good herb to grow in a window box.

HARDY ANNUAL.
HEIGHT AND SPREAD 2 ft (60 cm) by 1 ft (30 cm).
FLOWERS Tiny white flowers held in umbels (flowerheads on stalks that grow from a single stalk).
FLOWERING Spring to summer.
SOIL Light, fertile soil that does not dry out.
SITE Partial shade.
PROPAGATION Sow seed in spring and late summer where the plants are to grow. Thin plants to 6 in (15 cm) apart and water regularly during the summer. Seed sown in early spring will mature in the summer. In warm areas, seed sown in late summer will produce winter leaves.
USES Culinary.
OTHER VARIETIES AND SPECIES
A. cerefolium 'Brussels Winter', *A. sylvestris* (Cow parsley).

LEFT Anethum graveolens, *dill, is an attractive plant with its broad, yellow flowerheads. It is a popular herb in the kitchen, with a distinctive taste. Its strongly flavored seeds are often used in baking.*

Arctostaphylos uva-ursi
Bearberry

The bearberry is an attractive evergreen shrub of great importance in herbal medicine. It is used to treat bladder and kidney infections but, as with all medicinal herbs, on no account should any part of the plant be used at home. It needs acid soil to flourish and can be grown in a container with conifers or in the garden, used as a ground-cover plant in acid soil. Being evergreen, the leaves remain interesting throughout the winter.

HARDY (Zone 2).
HEIGHT AND SPREAD 6 in (15 cm) by 2 ft (60 cm).
FLOWERS Small pink-tipped white flowers held on terminal clusters followed by bright scarlet berries in fall.
FLOWERING Early summer.
FOLIAGE Dark green, shiny, spoon-shaped leaves carried on long trailing shoots.
SOIL Light, acid, humus-rich.
SITE Partial shade.
PROPAGATION Layer in summer. Take softwood cuttings in summer.
USES Medicinal.
OTHER VARIETIES AND SPECIES
A. glandulosa, *A. stanfordiana*, *A. uva-ursi* 'Massachusetts', *A. u-u.* 'Vancouver Jade'.

Armeria maritima
Thrift

An ideal perennial plant for the front of a trough or container, sea thrift produces masses of pink flowers held aloft on stalks springing from a dense clump. It is a common seaside flower and flourishes in dry places and poor soil. The flowers have a delicate scent of honey. Formerly a medicinal herb, an infusion of the fresh or dried flowers was used as an antiseptic and to treat nervous disorders and obesity.

CAUTION Thrift is thought to cause an allergic reaction and is no longer used in herbal medicine.

HARDY (Zone 4).
HEIGHT AND SPREAD 6–12 in (15–30 cm)
FLOWERS The flowerheads form dense balls, rose pink, occasionally white.
FLOWERING Summer.
FOLIAGE Short, narrow, dark green leaves forming a clump.
SOIL Well drained, light, sandy.
SITE Open, sunny.
PROPAGATION Sow seeds in fall. Take semi-ripe cuttings or divide in summer.
USES Formerly medicinal, dried flowers.
OTHER VARIETIES AND SPECIES
A. maritima 'Alba', *A. m.* 'Düsseldorfer Stolz', *A. m.* 'Splendens', *A. m.* 'Vindictive.

Arnica montana
Arnica

Also called mountain tobacco, arnica is a much-valued perennial herb in medicine and arnica ointment is used to treat bruises and sprains. It is also used in homeopathy to treat epilepsy, high blood pressure and shock. As with all medicinal herbs, it should not be used in its natural state for the plant is poisonous and toxic and can cause skin irritation. It is not a large plant and carries attractive yellow flowers. It is a popular plant for growing in containers.

HARDY (Zone 3).
HEIGHT AND SPREAD 1–2 ft (30–60 cm) by 6 in (15 cm).
FLOWERS Golden-yellow daisy-like, held on a long stem.
FLOWERING Midsummer to early fall.
FOLIAGE Held in a basal rosette of four to eight downy leaves.
SOIL Humus-rich, sandy, acid.
SITE Open, sunny.
PROPAGATION Sow seeds in fall in a cold frame. Divide in spring.
USES Medicinal.
OTHER VARIETIES AND SPECIES
A. chamissonis, *A. sachalinensis*.

LEFT *Chervil is another popular culinary herb and was formerly used to flavor many soups and stews. It is a good herb for a shady spot.*

Artemisia dracunculus
French Tarragon, Estragon

This herbaceous perennial is often used in the kitchen, particularly to flavor vinegar, and was historically used to cure toothache. The leaves are also used in salads and as a seasoning. Grown as a kitchen herb, the leaves can be cut and used when young. Alternatively cut off the flowerheads as they form and then cut and dry the stems for use during the fall and winter. Strip the leaves from the plant when drying is complete and store them in airtight bottles. French tarragon is not totally hardy and protection may be needed over winter in cold regions.

CAUTION: Artemisia is potentially toxic; only use *A. dracunculus* or
A. d. dracunculoides (Russian tarragon).

HARDY (Zones 4–5).
HEIGHT AND SPREAD 2–3 ft (60–90 cm) by 2 ft (60 cm).
FLOWERS Insignificant, white or gray.
FLOWERING Summer.
SOIL Light, well drained.
SITE Sunny.
PROPAGATION Divide roots in spring or take softwood cuttings in summer.
USES Culinary.
OTHER VARIETIES AND SPECIES
A. abrotanum (southernwood),
A. absinthium (wormwood).

Artemisia vulgaris
Mugwort, St John's Herb

One of the oldest perennial herbs, mugwort is used in herbal medicine to cure stomach ailments and treat menstrual disorders. It is also used in insect repellents, Chinese medicine and from time to time in the kitchen as a flavoring in meat dishes although it is rarely used this way nowadays. It is only suitable in a container garden with a good deal of room, because the plant reaches 6 ft (1.8 m) high and should be planted at the back of any container. The name comes from the Greek goddess Artemis.

HARDY (Zone 4).
HEIGHT 6 ft (1.8 m).
FLOWERS Small, reddish-brown.
FLOWERING Late summer.
SOIL Light, well drained.
SITE Open and sunny.
PROPAGATION Sow seed *in situ* in spring or take cuttings in summer.
USES Medicinal, culinary.
OTHER VARIETIES AND SPECIES
A. dracunculus (tarragon), *A. absinthium* (wormwood), *A. abrotanum* (southernwood).

Atriplex hortensis
var. *rubra*
Red Mountain Spinach, Red Orache

With its dark red stems and leaves and attractive small spikes of red flowers, red mountain spinach is a good herb to grow as a focal point in a container or herb garden. It grows to a height of 5 ft (1.5 m). It was formerly much grown as a vegetable and also used in herbal medicine to treat sore throats and jaundice. If the plant is to be used as a vegetable, it is advisable to pick the leaves when they are young as the older ones become tough. Cook them the same way as spinach. If the plant is allowed to mature, the stems can be cut and used in dried flower arrangements.

HALF-HARDY ANNUAL.
HEIGHT AND SPREAD 5 ft (1.5 m) by 2 ft (60 cm).
FLOWERS Small red or green spikes of flowers, depending on the species grown.
FLOWERING Summer to early fall.
SOIL Moist, well drained.
SITE Open, sunny.
PROPAGATION Sow seed in spring when the soil temperature has reached 50°F (10°C). Thin plants to 18 in (45 cm). Water in dry periods to prevent bolting.
USES Culinary, formerly medicinal, dried flowers.
OTHER VARIETIES AND SPECIES
A. hortensis, *A. h.* green-leaved,
A. h. gold-leaved.

LEFT *Mugwort,* Artemisia, *has been used for centuries in herbal medicine and as an insect repellent. It was also sometimes used as a culinary herb for flavoring meat dishes.*

RIGHT *In midsummer calamint puts on a vibrant display of pink flowers.*

Calamintha grandiflora
Garden Calamint

Also known as mountain balm, garden calamint is an attractive, small bushy perennial with mint-scented leaves. It has been cultivated in gardens since the 16th century. An extract of the leaves and shoots was formerly used in medicine in cases of fever, because the plant has diaphoretic (sweat-inducing) properties, and as an expectorant. In the famous herbal of John Gerard, the herbalist and barber-surgeon, first published in 1597, calamint was recommended as a cure for melancholy. An infusion made from fresh or dried leaves is a pleasant tonic.

HARDY (Zones 4–5).
HEIGHT AND SPREAD 18 in (45 cm).
FLOWERS Drooping pink multiple heads of up to five flowers each.
FLOWERING Midsummer.
FOLIAGE Ovate, toothed, downy.
SOIL Well drained.
SITE Partial shade.
PROPAGATION Sow seeds in spring in a cold frame, divide in spring.
USES Medicinal.
OTHER VARIETIES AND SPECIES
C. alpina, C. cretica, C. nepeta,
C. n. 'White Cloud', *C. n.* 'Blue Cloud'.

Bellis perennis
Daisy

Most people think of daisies as weeds found in lawns, but they are attractive and decorative perennial plants. Varieties in many shades of white, pink and red can be grown as edging plants to add color and interest to the container garden. In medieval times, the daisy was sometimes called bruisewort and used as a poultice but it is only used infrequently in homeopathic medicine today. In the kitchen, the young leaves can be added to salads and the flowers used as decoration.

HARDY (Zone 3).
HEIGHT AND SPREAD 3 in (7.5 cm) by 6 in (15 cm).
FLOWERS The common *Bellis perennis* has white flowers tinged with pink and yellow centers. Cultivars come in all shades of pink, white and red.
FLOWERING Spring to summer.
SOIL Any reasonably fertile, well drained.
SITE Sun or partial shade.
PROPAGATION Sow seeds in spring or summer.
USES Medicinal, culinary.
OTHER VARIETIES AND SPECIES
B. p. Goliath Mixed (large double flowers), *B. p.* Pomponette Series (double flowers to 1½ in/4 cm across).

Borago officinalis
Borage, Bugloss

Borage is a favorite herb for flavoring summer drinks, especially fruit and wine cups; the delicate blue flowers add a cucumber taste. The leaves can be eaten in salads and the flowers added as decoration. They can also be candied or fried in batter. Borage is also a medicinal herb often used in the treatment of coughs, colds and depression.

HARDY ANNUAL.
HEIGHT AND SPREAD 2–3 ft (60–90 cm) by 18 in (45 cm).
FLOWERS Bright blue, star-shaped five-petalled flowers that turn pink with age.
FLOWERING Summer.
FOLIAGE Dull green leaves that give off a cucumber scent. They are exceptionally hairy.
SOIL Fertile, well drained.
SITE Open, sunny.
PROPAGATION Sow seeds in late spring. The plants will need staking. Thin the seedlings to 1 ft (30 cm) apart. Borage has a long tap root, so plant in a deep container.
USES Culinary, medicinal.
OTHER VARIETIES AND SPECIES
B. officinalis 'Alba' (white flowers), *B. pygmaea.*

Calendula officinalis
Calendula, Pot Marigold

Pot marigolds are one of the most colorful of all perennial herbs and among the easiest to grow. They used to be grown as a vegetable but have fallen from favor as the leaves are rather bitter. Young leaves can be used in salads and the flowers can be sprinkled on salads and soups as decoration. They can also be dried and used as a coloring or a substitute for saffron. Medicinally, calendula was used as an antiseptic and to treat gangrene.

HARDY (Zone 3), usually grown as an annual.
HEIGHT AND SPREAD 1–2 ft (30–60 cm) by 18 in (45 cm).
FLOWERS Pale to deep orange, rather like large orange daisies.
FLOWERING Summer.
FOLIAGE Pale green, pointed or spoon-shaped hairy leaves.
SOIL Most garden soils.
SITE Sunny.
PROPAGATION Sow seeds *in situ* in spring. Thin seedlings to 6 in (15 cm) apart.
USES Culinary, medicinal, dye plant.
OTHER VARIETIES AND SPECIES Many cultivars including
C. officinalis Bon Bon Series, C. o. Pacific Beauty Series, C. o. Prince Series.

Cardamine pratensis
Lady's Smock, Cuckoo Flower

Another common name for this perennial plant is bitter cress, which gives a clue to its uses in the kitchen; it was also used as a medicinal herb. It has a pleasant, slightly hot flavor when used in salads. The name is derived from the Greek *cardia*, meaning heart, and it was believed to be good for heart troubles. It is one of the most common wildflowers and occurs naturally in moist sites in Europe and North America.

HARDY (Zone 3).
HEIGHT AND SPREAD 12 in (30 cm) by 9 in (23 cm).
FLOWERS Purple, lilac or white flowers held aloft on panicles.
FLOWERING Spring to early summer.
FOLIAGE Lower leaves are rounded or kidney-shaped and form a rosette. The upper leaves are narrow.
SOIL Moist loam.
SITE Partial shade.
PROPAGATION Sow seed in a cold frame in summer or fall and plant out in spring. Divide plants after flowering or take cuttings in late summer and grow in a cold frame over winter.
USES Medicinal, culinary.
OTHER VARIETIES AND SPECIES
C. pratensis 'Flore Pleno' (double flowered), C. trifolia.

Carum carvi
Caraway

Caraway, a small biennial plant that belongs to the carrot family, is very similar to dill and fennel. It has small white flowerheads and fine feathery, fern-like foliage. The leaves can be cut when young and eaten in salads, but a more common culinary use is the addition of the dried seeds to flavor cakes, bread and cooked meats.

HARDY (Zones 3–4).
HEIGHT AND SPREAD 12–30 in (30–75 cm) by 12 in (30 cm).
FLOWERS Small and white.
FLOWERING Summer.
FOLIAGE Fern-like, fine, green.
SOIL Light, well drained.
SITE Full sun.
PROPAGATION Sow seeds in late summer *in situ*. Thin to 6 in (15 cm) apart. The plant will carry flowerheads and seeds in its second year.
OTHER VARIETIES AND SPECIES None.

RIGHT *Both the flowers and leaves of calendula can be used in the kitchen. This colorful plant was also traditionally used as an antiseptic.*

LEFT *Cornflowers have delicate, vibrantly colored flowerheads which are enduringly popular in flower arrangements.*

Chamaemelum nobile
Lawn Chamomile, Roman Chamomile

Lawn chamomile is the perennial used to make chamomile lawns. Its leaves release a lovely apple scent when stepped on. The variety 'Treneague' is non-flowering and does not require cutting. Chamomile is also used as a herb tea and chamomile lotion is a soothing treatment for bites and stings. The flowers are also used in the preparation of hair tonics. Chamomile can be grown in a container as a covering plant and the small, white, daisy-like flowers make an attractive contrast in a green herb garden.

HARDY (Zones 3–4).
HEIGHT AND SPREAD 12 in (30 cm) spreading.
FLOWERS White daisy-like flowers with yellow centers held on single stems.
FLOWERING Summer.
FOLIAGE Low-growing, green and feathery.
SOIL Well drained, fertile.
SITE Sun or partial shade.
PROPAGATION Sow seeds *in situ* in spring, divide in spring.
USES Medicinal, scented lawns.
OTHER VARIETIES AND SPECIES
C. nobile 'Flore Pleno' (double white flowers).

Centaurea cyanus
Bachelor's Button

The annual cornflower is commercially grown for use by florists but a few sown in a container will provide a brilliant blue focal point in a patio garden. Cornflowers have the thistle-like head of their group and this makes a decorative seed-head much used in flower arrangements. A decoction of the flowerheads was formerly used as an eye wash and the plant also provides a blue dye. Modern varieties are available in mixed colors and dwarf forms.

HARDY ANNUAL.
HEIGHT AND SPREAD 1–3 ft (30–90 cm) by 8 in (20 cm).
FLOWERS Deep blue, thistle-like with a dark center.
FLOWERING Summer.
FOLIAGE Gray-green, thin, lance-like leaves.
SOIL Fertile, well drained.
SITE Open, sunny.
PROPAGATION Sow seeds outdoors in fall. Thin out in the spring.
USES Cut and dried flowers, medicinal, dye plant.
OTHER VARIETIES AND SPECIES
C. cyanus Frosty Mixed, *C. c.* 'Blue Diadem', *C. c.* Polka Dot Mixed.

Centaurea scabiosa
Greater Knapweed

A relative of the cornflower, greater knapweed is a hardy perennial plant whose striking, pink, thistle-like heads are much valued in flower arranging. The plant also has medicinal properties and was formerly used to heal wounds and soothe sore throats and coughs. It needs a good deal of room and if grown in a container you should take care not to crowd it too much with other plants. It forms a good focal point on a patio and gives color at the end of the summer when many other flowering plants are past their prime.

HARDY (Zone 3).
HEIGHT AND SPREAD 1–3 ft (30–90 cm) by 2 ft (60 cm).
FLOWERS Purple-crimson, thistle-like.
FLOWERING Late summer.
FOLIAGE Dull green, rounded lower leaves with thin upper leaves.
SOIL Can be grown in most soils.
SITE Open, sunny.
PROPAGATION Sow seeds in a cold frame in spring. Divide in spring. Self-seeds and may need containment.
USES Dried flowers, formerly medicinal.
OTHER VARIETIES AND SPECIES
C. dealbata, C. hypoleuca, C. nigra, C. simplicicaulis.

Consolida ajacis syn. Consolida ambigua
Larkspur

The annual larkspur, a close relative of the delphinium, is a well known plant that was formerly used in herbal medicine. However the plant is poisonous, particularly the seeds, and should not be taken in any form. The flowers are grown for their colors and for use as dried flowers, and the dried stems and seedheads are particularly attractive. The dwarf series is the most suitable for growing in containers, where the flowers can provide a lovely display of mixed colors in summer.

HARDY ANNUAL.
HEIGHT AND SPREAD 1–3 ft (30–90 cm) by 12–18 in (30–45 cm), depending on the variety.
FLOWERS Blue, purple, white and pink held on erect spikes.
FLOWERING Summer.
FOLIAGE Dark green, feathery, finely divided.
SOIL Fertile, well drained. They will not flourish in damp conditions.
SITE Open, sunny.
PROPAGATION Sow seeds *in situ* in fall in mild climates or spring; fall-sown seeds flower earlier and
provide better plants.
USES Cut and dried flowers.
OTHER VARIETIES AND SPECIES
C. ajacis Dwarf Rocket Series, *C. a.* Dwarf Hyacinth Series.

RIGHT Coriander, also known as cilantro, has been used as a spice for over 3000 years. The flowers are white with a pinkish tinge.

Coriandrum sativum
Coriander

Coriander is both an attractive plant in the garden and a favorite spice in the kitchen. The leaves and seeds are used in a wide range of Indian and Asian dishes. The herb is also used medicinally and reputedly aids digestion and contributes to longevity and an improved love-life. Coriander is not the most suitable herb for containers, because it has a long tap root (sometimes eaten as a vegetable itself), and care must be taken where it is planted. Sow seeds in succession throughout the summer to ensure a regular supply of fresh leaves. When the flowers die the seeds form; these are dried and ground as a spice.

ANNUAL.
HEIGHT AND SPREAD 1–2 ft (30–60 cm) by 9 in (23 cm).
FLOWERS Small white and pink flowers on flat heads.
FLOWERING Summer.
FOLIAGE Aromatic leaves; the lower leaves are bright green, shiny and stalked, the upper leaves are narrower and more divided.
SOIL Fertile, well drained.
SITE Full sun.
PROPAGATION Sow seed in spring and early summer and thin to 6 in (15 cm) apart.
USES Culinary, medicinal.
OTHER VARIETIES AND SPECIES
C. sativum 'Cilantro', *C. s.* 'Morocco', *C. s.* 'Santo'.

Crocus sativus
Saffron Crocus

The perennial bulb, saffron crocus, that bears lilac flowers in the fall is a lovely plant to grow in containers. However, the amount of saffron that one plant produces is minuscule – around 2000 plants are needed to produce 1 oz (28 g) – so the ordinary gardener should grow the bulb for decoration rather than the expensive yellow dye and scent used in cooking.

FROST-HARDY (Zone 6).
HEIGHT AND SPREAD 6 in (15 cm).
FLOWERS Pale lilac with dark veins and bright orange stigma.
FLOWERING Fall.
FOLIAGE Fine grasslike leaves that usually emerge shortly after the flowers.
SOIL Does best in poor, well drained soil.
SITE Sun or partial shade.
PROPAGATION Plant bulbs in late summer and divide clumps after flowering.
USES Culinary, dye plant.
OTHER VARIETIES AND SPECIES
Other fall-flowering crocuses include *C. banaticus, C. nudiflorus, C. serotinus*. There are also many cultivars.

Cymbopogon citratus
Lemon Grass

Native to India, this coarse perennial ornamental grass has lemon-scented leaves used in oriental cookery and, formerly, as an ingredient in herbal medicines and cosmetics. The narrow blue-green leaves can be cut and used fresh or dried and ground into a powder. The name comes from the Greek, *kymbe*, a boat, and *pogon*, a beard, a reference to the shape of the calyx. The leaves can be infused as a tea, and the essential oil, lemon-grass oil, is used in cosmetics as a skin cleanser.

HALF-HARDY (Zones 8–10).
HEIGHT AND SPREAD 2–3 ft
(60–90 cm).
FLOWERS Small greenish-white grass-like flowers are borne on terminal spikes or racemes.
FOLIAGE Narrow blue-green leaves, turning brown when dried.
SOIL Fertile, well drained.
SITE Will not survive frost and is best moved into a greenhouse or sunroom in winter. Can be placed outside in a warm sunny spot when the danger of frosts has passed.
PROPAGATION Sow seed at 55–64°F (13–18°C) in early spring. Propagation is usually by division in late spring.
USES Culinary, medicinal.
OTHER VARIETIES AND SPECIES
C. martinii (ginger grass), *C. nardus* (citronella grass).

Daucus carota
Queen Anne's Lace

Wild carrot was used in herbal medicine as a treatment for kidney disorders and urinary troubles, especially kidney stones. A decoction of the seed is used in cases of indigestion. It should not be taken during pregnancy. It is a hardy biennial that grows naturally in the wild, usually beside the sea or open fields, and has attractive white flowerheads that are sometimes tinged with pink or purple. The seedheads can be cut and dried to make winter decorations.

HARDY (Zone 5).
HEIGHT AND SPREAD 3 ft (90 cm) by 12 in (30 cm).
FLOWERS Compound, white, flat or convex flowerheads.
FLOWERING Midsummer.
FOLIAGE Medium green, finely divided and feathery.
SOIL Well drained, sandy loam.
SITE Full sun.
PROPAGATION Sow seed in spring, self-seeds.
USES Medicinal, dried flower arrangements.
OTHER VARIETIES AND SPECIES
The many varieties of carrot grown in the kitchen garden.

Dianthus caryophyllus
Clove Pink

It is a good idea to grow some pinks at the front of a container if you have a sunny site and enough room. They are attractive, deliciously scented perennial flowers, especially the old-fashioned varieties. The flowers of the clove pink *D. caryophyllus* can be used to make cordials, flavor drinks and decorate soups and salads. Pinks flourish on light alkaline soil in a sunny positions and do not need too fertile a soil. They do not like being waterlogged during the winter, so container-grown pinks need well-drained soil mix and little added fertilizer.

HARDY (borderline) (Zone 6).
HEIGHT AND SPREAD 2 ft (60 cm) by 18 in (45 cm).
FLOWERS Rose pink. Other varieties have flowers in the color range red to white.
FLOWERING Summer.
FOLIAGE Gray-green thin spiky leaves on many thin stems.
SOIL Light, alkaline.
SITE Open, sunny.
PROPAGATION Sow seed or take cuttings or pipings (a method peculiar to pinks and carnations where the central portion of a shoot is pulled out and the bottom leaves removed).
USES Culinary.
OTHER VARIETIES AND SPECIES
D. barbatus, D. chinensis, D. deltoides, D. superbus.

LEFT *Although larkspur is poisonous and should not be eaten, its dramatic purple spikes make a beautiful summer display.*

Echinacea purpurea
Purple Coneflower

This important perennial medicinal herb is native to North America, where the dried, powdered root was used by the Plains Indians as an antibiotic to cure rabies, snakebite and septicaemia. Today it is used in homeopathic medicine and is thought to have beneficial effects, boosting the immune system. With their petals radiating from a prominent center, coneflowers are rather like giant daisies, to which family they belong. The name comes from the Greek word *echinops* ("hedgehog"), an allusion to the bristles on the flower bracts.

HARDY (Zones 3–9).
HEIGHT AND SPREAD 1–2 ft (30–60 cm) by 9 in (23 cm).
FLOWERS Purple-pink daisy-like flowers with a prominent golden-brown cone-shaped center.
FOLIAGE Dull green, oval, toothed hairy basal leaves and long lance-shaped, toothed stem leaves. The stems are green tinted with red.
SOIL Fertile, well drained, moisture retentive.
SITE Sun or partial shade.
PROPAGATION Sow seed in spring at 55°F (13°C). Divide in spring or take root cuttings in late fall.
USES Medicinal.
OTHER VARIETIES AND SPECIES
E. purpurea 'Leuchstern', *E. p.* 'Magnus', *E. p.* 'White Lustre'.

Echium vulgare
Viper's Bugloss

An old biennial medicinal herb with violet-blue flowers that has several uses in the kitchen and is a spectacular sight in summer. It has a long taproot and should only be planted in deep containers. In olden times the plant was used as a poultice in cases of snakebite. The markings resemble the features of a snake. The flowers are mildly antiseptic and may be added to drinks or candied and the leaves can also be cooked as a vegetable. They taste a bit like spinach.

HARDY (Zone 5).
HEIGHT AND SPREAD 18–24 in (45–60 cm) by 12 in (30 cm).
FLOWERS Brilliant blue (pinkish violet in bud) carried on short spikes.
FLOWERING Early to midsummer.
FOLIAGE Bristly, lance-shaped, gray-green leaves.
SOIL Light, well drained.
SITE Full sun.
PROPAGATION Sow seeds in late spring. They need a temperature of 55–61°F (13–16°C) to germinate.
USES Formerly medicinal, culinary.
OTHER VARIETIES AND SPECIES
E. vulgare 'Blue Bedder' (light blue flowers), *E. v.* Dwarf Hybrids (18 in/45 cm) (pink, blue and white flowers).

Eschscholzia californica
California Poppy

Like many poppies the California poppy has narcotic qualities and was formerly used by the North American Indians as a remedy for toothache. They are attractive flowers. They have the merit of growing in the poorest soils and will survive in gravel. They self-seed freely. They can be sown directly into the container where you want them to grow and make excellent cut flowers.

ANNUAL.
HEIGHT AND SPREAD 1–2 ft (30–60 cm) by 6 in (15 cm).
FLOWERS Many colored four-petalled, poppy-shaped flowers, in the range pale yellow to orange, sometimes red and white.
FLOWERING Summer.
FOLIAGE Gray-green mat-forming, finely cut and sparse.
SOIL Poor, well drained.
SITE Open, sunny.
PROPAGATION Sow seed *in situ* in spring or in fall in mild climates.
USES Medicinal, cut flowers.
OTHER VARIETIES AND SPECIES
E. californica 'Ballerina', *E. c.* 'Dali', *E. c.* Thai Silk Series.

RIGHT Echinacea purpurea *(purple coneflower) is widely used as an ingredient in homeopathic remedies.*

Filipendula ulmaria
Meadowsweet

A most important perennial herb common in damp meadows. It was formerly used in medicine because the flowerheads contain salicylic acid from which aspirin is made. In medieval times it was a popular treatment for many of the illnesses associated with aspirin today. The leaves and root of the plant were also used as a dye. Tea can be made from the leaves to reduce fever and the dried flowers are used to flavor beer and drinks. Meadowsweet is an attractive plant with creamy white, sweet-smelling flowerheads and deeply divided dark green leaves.

HARDY (Zone 3).
HEIGHT AND SPREAD 2–3 ft (60–90 cm) by 18 in (45 cm).
FLOWERS Creamy white small fragrant flowers held on terminal clusters.
FLOWERING Early to late summer.
FOLIAGE Dark green above with white and downy underneath.
SOIL Rich, moisture retentive.
SITE Sun, partial shade.
PROPAGATION Sow seeds in fall or spring at 10–13°C (50–55°C). Divide plants in spring.
USES Medicinal, culinary, dye plant.
OTHER VARIETIES AND SPECIES
F. ulmaria 'Aurea', F. u. 'Multiplex', F. vulgaris.

LEFT *Meadowsweet was a popular remedy in medieval times for many ailments that are now treated with aspirin..*

Galium odoratum
Sweet Woodruff

An attractive small ground-covering perennial that can be raised in containers in shade or partial shade. Another common name for the plant is bedstraw and the leaves used to be cut and placed between sheets becaue they give off a pleasant smell of new-mown hay. The plant has bright green leaves and tiny attractive white star-shaped flowers. It is an important medicinal herb and is used to treat glandular fever and eczema. It is also made into a herbal tea to cure stomach ache and is used in pot pourris and perfumes.

HARDY (Zone 3).
HEIGHT AND SPREAD 12 in (30 cm), spreading.
FLOWERS Small white star-shaped, fragrant, held in clusters.
FLOWERING Early summer.
FOLIAGE Bright green, small lance-shaped leaves held in clusters.
SOIL Rich, moisture retentive.
SITE Shade or partial shade.
PROPAGATION Sow seed in late summer. The seed will germinate the following spring. Divide in summer.
USES Medicinal, scented plant.
OTHER VARIETIES AND SPECIES
G. mollugo, G. verum, Asperula perpusilla.

Geranium robertianum
Herb Robert

For many gardeners this plant is an unwanted weed that spreads over paths, but it has a certain charm. It can be grown in a container of medicinal herbs, as a backdrop for other plants. In the Middle Ages it was considered to have magic properties and was a common treatment for wounds. It is still used in herbal medicine as a treatment for sore throats and mouth ulcers. The plant has a strange, rather unpleasant smell.

HARDY ANNUAL OR BIENNIAL (Zone 5).
HEIGHT AND SPREAD 6–18 in (15–45 cm) by 12 in (30 cm).
FLOWERS Small rose-pink five-petalled flowers with white centers and red spots.
FLOWERING Summer.
FOLIAGE Finely cut fragile green red-tinged leaves carried on bright red stalks.
SOIL Moisture retentive.
SITE Any.
PROPAGATION Sow seeds in late fall or spring, self-seeds.
USES Medicinal.
OTHER VARIETIES AND SPECIES
G. pratense, G. maculatum, G. sylvaticum and many others.

Geum urbanum
Herb Bennet

Another perennial "weed" that has attractive flowers and foliage and was long used in herbal medicine. Herb bennet is closely related to a number of attractive perennials often found in herbaceous borders. The wild herb bennet has a fairly large thick, pink root that was formerly dried and ground and used to cure stomach and liver complaints or made into a tea to reduce fever. The young leaves of the plant can be eaten in salads. Another common name for the plant was clove root and the root was used as a flavoring in many dishes.

HARDY (Zone 3).
HEIGHT AND SPREAD 1–2 ft (30–60 cm) by 12 in (30 cm).
FLOWERS Small yellow flowers held in loose panicles.
FLOWERING Summer.
FOLIAGE Dark green oval rosetted, the largest leaves are at the base, deeply lobed.
SOIL Fertile, moisture retentive.
SITE Sun or partial shade.
PROPAGATION Sow seed *in situ* in spring.
USES Medicinal, culinary.
OTHER VARIETIES AND SPECIES
G. rivale (Water avens), *G. triflorum.*

Helianthus annuus
Sunflower

Attempt to grow sunflowers in containers only if you have a sunny patio and wall to which the plants can be secured. They are spectacular plants and much appreciated by children. The seeds can be dried and used to feed parrots and other birds. Sunflower seeds grown commercially are made into oil. The plant has to be kept well watered and the heads should be cut and dried when they start to droop. Plant waste is high in potash and should be added to the compost heap.

ANNUAL.
HEIGHT AND SPREAD 10–15 ft (3–6 m) by 18 in (45 cm). Plants grown in containers may be a bit smaller.
FLOWERS Large flowers with yellow rays and a brown-gold center made up of many small flowers. These form the seeds.
FLOWERING Mid- to late summer.
FOLIAGE Large, stalked, green, hairy leaves.
SOIL Any but the plant must be kept well watered.
SITE Full sun.
PROPAGATION Sow seed in spring at 61°F (16°C).
USES Culinary.
OTHER VARIETIES AND SPECIES
H. annuum 'Autumn Beauty', *H. a.* 'Russian Giant'.

Helichrysum italicum
ssp. *serotinum*
Curry Plant

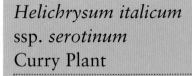

An evergreen subshrub with thin silver-gray leaves and small yellow flowers. In the garden it is used as an edging plant but can be grown in containers as a focal plant in a group of herbs. The leaves and flowers are intensely aromatic and give off the smell of curry when brushed against. Some people recommend it as a flavoring but this is not really a good idea because the plant is not connected with curry in the true sense of the word and if consumed sometimes causes an adverse reaction. The flowers can be cut and dried for use in flower arranging or used in pot pourri. It has to be grown in well-drained soil so it requires little water if grown in a container over winter.

HARDY (borderline) (Zone 6).
HEIGHT AND SPREAD 2 ft (60 cm) by 2 ft (60 cm).
FLOWERS Small deep yellow on long stalks.
FLOWERING Summer.
FOLIAGE Silver-gray, narrow leaves.
SOIL Any well drained.
SITE Full sun.
PROPAGATION Take softwood or semi-ripe cuttings in summer.
USES Dried flowers.
OTHER VARIETIES AND SPECIES
H. italicum, H. petiolare, H. splendidum.

LEFT *The tall silver-gray leaves and stems of the curry plant make a good focal point in a container of lower-growing herbs.*

Heliotropium arborescens
Heliotrope

A native of Peru, the heliotrope or cherry pie is usually grown as a half-hardy annual in temperate climates. In its native habitat it grows into a bushy shrub and it is valued for its scent. It is a good plant to grow in a container for it needs a minimum winter temperature of 45°F (7°C) and it can be brought inside and given protection over the winter months. The flowers are extremely fragrant and used to scent pot pourris and the plant was formerly used in homeopathic medicine. The flowers are said to turn towards the sun and this gives the plant its name from the Greek, *helios* (sun) and *trope* (turning).

HALF-HARDY (Zones 8–10), usually grown as an annual.
HEIGHT AND SPREAD 2 ft (60 cm).
FLOWERS Purple or lavender-blue, borne in flat clusters.
FLOWERING Summer.
FOLIAGE Dark green, sometimes purple-tinged, glossy.
SOIL Fertile, well drained.
SITE Full sun.
PROPAGATION Sow seeds in spring at 61–64°F (16–18°C). Take semi-ripe or stem-tip cuttings in summer.
USES Perfume, pot pourri, formerly medicinal.
OTHER VARIETIES AND SPECIES
H. arborescens 'Chatsworth',
H. a. 'Marine', *H. a.* 'Regal Dwarf'.

RIGHT *Any pot pourri will benefit from the addition of the dried petals of the highly fragrant Heliotrope.*

Hesperis matronalis
Sweet Rocket

Also known as Dame's Violet this is an old-fashioned, short-lived, perennial or biennial that can be found in many cottage borders. It has attractive terminal spikes of four-petalled white, purple or violet flowers and the narrow leaves can be picked and used in salads. It grows best in fertile soil so if you grow it in a container make sure that the soil mix has added fertilizer. The flowers are scented particularly in the evening. The name comes from the Greek *hesperos*, an allusion to this.

HARDY (borderline) (Zone 6).
HEIGHT AND SPREAD 3 ft (90 cm) by 18 in (45 cm).
FLOWERS White, purple or violet.
FLOWERING Summer.
FOLIAGE Dark green, oval pointed leaves.
SOIL Prefers rich, moisture retentive.
SITE Sun or partial shade.
PROPAGATION Sow seeds *in situ* in spring. Thin to 18 in (45 cm) apart.
USES Culinary, evening scent.
OTHER VARIETIES AND SPECIES
H. matronalis 'Alba Plena',
H. m. 'Lilacina Flore Plena'.

Humulus lupulus
Hop

The hop is a good plant to grow in a container provided that a wall can offer it some support. A vigorous perennial climber, it will cover a trellis in summer or grow over a pergola. The leaves are attractive. The variety 'Aureus' with its golden leaves is the one most commonly grown. Buy female plants rather than attempt to grow hops from seed because they are technically dioecious which means that the male and female plants are separate. Hops are used in brewing. They are a gentle sedative and can be used to stuff pillows or dried for winter flower arrangements.

HARDY (Zone 3).
HEIGHT 10–15 ft (3–4.5 m) depending on the variety grown.
FLOWERS Greenish-yellow hanging down in large loose cones.
FLOWERING Late summer.
FOLIAGE Dark green, 3 to 5-lobed leaves.
SOIL Rich, moisture retentive.
SITE Sunny.
PROPAGATION Sow seeds at 59–64°F (15–18°C) in spring or take softwood cuttings in spring.
USES Culinary, medicinal, dried flowers.
OTHER VARIETIES AND SPECIES
H. lupulus 'Aureus', *H. japonicus*.

Hyssopus officinalis
Hyssop

One of the oldest herbs in cultivation, hyssop is an attractive evergreen shrub with brilliant blue flowers held on a spike. It grows well with other scented herbs such as lavender and sage. The leaves can be used to make hyssop tea which is considered a cure for bronchitis and chest complaints but the leaves are more often used in soups, salads and stews to add a bittermint flavor. The flavor is strong and not universally popular. It was also used by the monks who made Chartreuse and Benedictine liqueurs and hyssop oil is used in perfumes. The plant is attractive to bees and butterflies.

HARDY (Zones 4–5).
HEIGHT AND SPREAD 2 ft (60 cm) by 18 in (45 cm).
FLOWERS Rich blue two-lipped flowers growing on spikes.
FLOWERING Summer.
FOLIAGE Dark green, narrow pointed aromatic leaves.
SOIL Light, well drained.
SITE Full sun.
PROPAGATION Sow seeds in fall, take softwood cuttings in summer.
USES Medicinal, culinary.
OTHER VARIETIES AND SPECIES
H. officinalis f. *albus*, *H. o.* ssp. *aristatus*, *H. o. roseus*.

RIGHT *Hyssop has been cultivated for centuries and used to impart its strong flavoring to soups and stews. Hyssop tea was also a traditional cure for chest complaints.*

Jasminum officinale
Jasmine

The common jasmine is a popular climber found on the walls of many gardens. Unlike a number of jasmines, common jasmine is deciduous although it may retain some leaves in mild winters. It is a good climber to grow in a container for it is vigorous and beautifully scented with attractive white flowers. The form *affine* was used in the perfume industry and jasmine tea made in China is made from green tea and jasmine flowers. *J. nudiflorum*, winter jasmine, has bright yellow flowers on bare stalks in the winter and gives the gardener hope for the summer to come.

HARDY (borderline) (Zone 6).
HEIGHT 6–16 ft (1.8–5 m).
FLOWERS Very fragrant white, star-shaped flowers in clusters.
FLOWERING Summer.
FOLIAGE Dark green, oval leaves divided into 5–9 leaflets.
SOIL Fertile, well drained.
SITE Sunny, sheltered.
PROPAGATION Semi-ripe cuttings in summer, layer in fall.
USES Perfume, tea, formerly medicinal.
OTHER VARIETIES AND SPECIES
J. nudiflorum (winter jasmine),
J. o. f. *affine*, *J. o.* 'Argenteovariegatum'.

Juniperus communis
Juniper

A number of junipers grow into fairly large evergreen trees up to 20 ft (6 m) high but there are many slow-growing dwarf forms that are most suitable for growing in containers. The best are *J. communis* 'Compressa' that only grows at the rate of 1 in (2–3 cm) a year and *J. c.* var. *depressa* which is prostrate. Junipers have loosely arranged needle-like leaves and green fruit that ripens over two to three years turning blue then black. This fruit contains the juniper berries used in cooking.

HARDY (Zone 5).
HEIGHT AND SPREAD 32 in (80 cm) by 18 in (45 cm).
FLOWERS Small yellow-green.
FLOWERING Early summer.
FOLIAGE Thin needle-like leaves blue green with a white band on the inner leaves.
SOIL Any.
SITE Full sun or partial shade.
PROPAGATION Grow from seed but germination may take five years.
USES Culinary.
OTHER VARIETIES AND SPECIES
J. c. 'Depressa Aurea' (yellow leaves) reaches 5 ft (1.5 m) wide by 2 ft (60 cm).

Laurus nobilis
Sweet Bay

In the wild or grown in a sheltered garden the bay tree can reach 12 m (40 ft) or more. Notwithstanding that, it is an excellent ornamental, evergreen tree for the container gardener and is found in pots and tubs in many town or country gardens. Bay trees have smooth pointed leaves that are dried and used to flavor stews and the leaves were traditionally used to crown returning victors from the wars in Ancient Rome. Bay trees are easy to grow and merely require feeding to promote healthy growth and clipping to shape once or twice a year. It is best to do this individually with secateurs as the severed leaves can look unsightly.

FROST-HARDY (Zones 6–7).
HEIGHT AND SPREAD Variable.
FLOWERS Small creamy yellow followed by black berries on mature plants.
FLOWERING Early summer.
FOLIAGE Dark green, smooth, pointed leaves.
SOIL Any well drained.
SITE Sun or partial shade.
PROPAGATION Sow seed in fall or take semi-ripe cuttings in summer.
USES Culinary.
OTHER VARIETIES AND SPECIES
L. nobilis f. *angustifolia*,
L. n. 'Aureus' (golden-yellow leaves).

Lavandula
Lavender

Lavender is a wonderfully scented evergreen shrub to grow in a container close to the house. It needs sun to show at its best. A low-growing variety can be used to fill a whole container or a selection can fringe a large container. Lavender was used as a medicinal herb in medieval times and is still used in infusions as a cure for coughs. Its chief use in the home is dried in pot pourris or in sachets for scent. Cut back plants hard in spring to within 1 in (2.5 cm) of last year's growth. Trim lightly after flowering to keep neat.

FROST-HARDY (Zones 5–8).
HEIGHT AND SPREAD To 3 ft (90 cm) depending on the variety grown.
FLOWERS Purple, blue, white or pink, held on long spikes in tight narrow heads.
FLOWERING Summer.
FOLIAGE Gray or gray-green thin leaves growing from a stem.
SOIL Well drained.
SITE Open, sunny.
PROPAGATION Seed in spring in a cold frame. Take semi-ripe cuttings in summer.
USES Scent, pot pourri, medicinal.
OTHER VARIETIES AND SPECIES
Low-growing lavenders include:
L. angustifolia 'Little Lady', *L. a.* 'Little Lottie', *L. a.* 'Imperial Gem',
L. a. 'Walberton's Silver Edge'.

Leucanthemum vulgare
Ox-eye Daisy

Commonly called the marguerite or moon daisy, the ox-eye daisy is a common perennial wildflower that can add attraction to any container garden. The young fresh leaves can be used in salads and it was formerly a herbal remedy in the treatment of coughs and catarrh. Externally it was applied to wounds and bruises. The plant self-seeds in the wild and care must be taken to remove unwanted seedlings if they are grown in containers.

HARDY (Zone 3).
HEIGHT AND SPREAD 1–2 ft (30–60 cm) by 1 ft (30 cm).
FLOWERS Daisy-like with a pronounced yellow center.
FLOWERING Early summer.
FOLIAGE Small, toothed, green leaves; those at the base of the plant are rounder than those on the stalks.
SOIL Fertile, well drained.
SITE Full sun.
PROPAGATION Sow seeds in late summer or spring. Divide plants after flowering.
USES Culinary, medicinal.
OTHER VARIETIES AND SPECIES
L. vulgare 'Maikönigin' ('May Queen'),
L. maximum.

RIGHT *Lavender can be cut and dried and used in pot pourris and in sachets to scent clothes in drawers and wardrobes.*

Levisticum officinale
Lovage

Only grow lovage if you have a good deal of room in the container garden because you may have to devote a whole container to just one plant. A perennial, it takes some years to reach these proportions. If it is a favorite herb and you wish to grow it, dig up and throw away the plant after two or three years and replant. The leaves of lovage can be used to flavor soups and stews, the stalks, but not the central flower stem, can be blanched and eaten and the seeds are also used to flavor bread. The taste is a bit like a peppery celery. As the name implies it was regarded as an aphrodisiac in medieval times and included in love potions. A tea made from the leaves is considered an aid to digestion.

HARDY (Zone 3).
HEIGHT AND SPREAD 4 ft (1.2 m) or more by 3 ft (90 cm).
FLOWERS Star-shaped, yellow-green, carried on flat heads. It is best to cut these off unless you wish to harvest the seed.
FLOWERING Midsummer.
FOLIAGE Dark green, shiny leaves shaped like celery. The leaves are very aromatic.
SOIL Rich, well drained, moisture retentive.
SITE Full sun.
PROPAGATION It is easiest to buy young plants from a nursery but if you want to raise your own, sow seeds in fall or spring. Mature plants can be divided in spring.
USES Culinary, medicinal.
OTHER VARIETIES AND SPECIES
Ligusticum scoticum (Scots lovage).

Matricaria recutita
Wild Chamomile

Also known as May weed, wild chamomile is a well-known wildflower found growing on the sides of the road and in alkaline soil in early summer. It has fragrant small white daisylike flowers with yellow centers. Wild chamomile is best known for chamomile tea, a calming drink, supposed to aid digestion. The essential oil was also used in hair tonic mostly as a shampoo or hair conditioner. The most commonly grown chamomiles are Roman chamomile, *Chamaemelum nobile* 'Flore Pleno' and *C. n.* 'Treneague', the non-flowering variety used for chamomile lawns. The plants self-seed rapidly and have to checked, otherwise they may become invasive.

ANNUAL.
HEIGHT AND SPREAD 18 in (45 cm) by 12 in (30 cm).
FLOWERS Small daisy-like flowers with prominent yellow centers borne on terminal clusters.
FLOWERING Early summer.
FOLIAGE Green feathery leaves.
SOIL Light, well drained.
SITE Open, sunny.
PROPAGATION Sow seed in spring.
USES Tea, perfumes.
OTHER VARIETIES AND SPECIES
Chamaemelum nobile 'Flore Pleno, *C.n.* 'Treneague'.

Melissa officinalis
Lemon Balm

This is an easy perennial to grow. It cannot be said to be very attractive although the variegated form 'All Gold' has blotched yellow and green leaves. The leaves are very fragrant with a pronounced lemony smell and can be used to flavor tea, soups, custards or wine cups. It was also much used in herbal medicine to treat colds, influenza and insomnia and to lower blood pressure. The small flowers are much loved by bees and the name comes from *melissa*, a bee.

HARDY (Zones 4–5).
HEIGHT AND SPREAD 2 ft (60 cm) by 18 in (45 cm).
FLOWERS Small pale yellow, white flowers on small spikes.
FLOWERING Midsummer.
FOLIAGE Light green heart-shaped rather rough leaves.
SOIL Fertile, well drained.
SITE Sun or partial shade.
PROPAGATION Division in spring.
USES Culinary, scent, bee plant.
OTHER VARIETIES AND SPECIES
M. officinalis 'All Gold', *M. o.* 'Aurea'.

RIGHT *The variegated leaves of* Melissa officinalis *can be used to add a lemon flavor to teas and soups.*

Mentha × piperita
Peppermint

Peppermint is used in flavoring and also in cosmetics and soaps. It is quite a large perennial and reaches 3 ft (90 cm) in height. It can be planted in containers where its red stems and crisp, red-tinted leaves look attractive. It is the most valuable of all the mints medicinally. Fields of peppermint are grown commercially, and the essential oils distilled for a number of uses. In England the center of the peppermint industry used to be the town of Mitcham in Surrey. The plant is a hybrid of *M. aquatica*, watermint, and *M. arvensis*, cornmint.

CAUTION All mints spread vigorously and do best in fertile, well-drained soil that retains moisture. They need to be contained. The traditional way of doing this in the garden was to plant them in an old bucket sunk into the soil with the bottom removed. If mint is grown in a container a smaller container, such as an old flower pot is most suitable for this.

Mints have hairy leaves which can cause skin irritations and rashes. Handle them with care. Similarly, don't drink mint tea continuously over a long period.

FROST-HARDY (Zone 5).
HEIGHT AND SPREAD 90 cm (3 ft) by 45 cm (18 in) or more.
FLOWERS Mauve or white held on long spikes.
FLOWERING Summer.
FOLIAGE Hairy, red-tinted, oval green leaves.
SOIL Well drained, moisture retentive.
SITE Open, sunny.
PROPAGATION Divide runners in fall. Never attempt to grow any mint from seed as the varieties are unlikely to breed true.
USES Culinary, medicinal, cosmetics.
OTHER VARIETIES AND SPECIES
M. × piperita citrata (eau de cologne mint, lemon mint), *M. aquatica* (watermint), *M. spicata* (spearmint).

LEFT *Pennyroyal was a popular medieval food flavoring, and it was also used to ward off fleas.*

Mentha pulegium
Pennyroyal,

Botanically mints are complicated because they hybridize freely and many natural varieties occur in various parts of the world. Pennyroyal may not be the most suitable perennial herb to grow in a container because it spreads quickly and is sometimes used in gardens for ground cover, but it is a deliciously pungent herb and was used in medieval times to conceal the taste of rotten meat and also in herbal medicines. It can be dried and used in the kitchen and it also helps to ward off fleas and to treat colds and insect bites.

HARDY (Zone 3).
HEIGHT AND SPREAD 8 in (20 cm) by 12 in (30 cm) or more.
FLOWERS Lilac-mauve flowers carried on erect spikes in dense whorls.
FLOWERING Summer.
FOLIAGE Dark green, oval.
SOIL Light, well drained.
SITE Sun, partial shade.
PROPAGATION Sow seeds under glass in spring. Divide plants in spring.
USES Culinary, medicinal.
OTHER VARIETIES AND SPECIES
M. × piperita, *M. requienii*.

Mentha spicata
Spearmint

The most commonly grown garden mint that is considered by many as the best for making mint sauce and for flavoring mint drinks in summer. Other favored perennial mints in the kitchen are *M. suavolens*, (apple mint) or its variety *M. s.* 'Variegata' that has attractive white and green leaves and *M. × villosa alopecuroides* Bowles' Mint, is a popular mint often used for flavoring new potatoes.

HARDY (Zone 5).
HEIGHT AND SPREAD 2 ft (60 cm) by 8 in (20 cm).
FLOWERS Cylindrical spikes of pink, white or lilac flowers in whorls.
FLOWERING Summer.
FOLIAGE Bright green, lance shaped.
SOIL Fertile, moisture retentive.
SITE Sun or partial shade.
PROPAGATION By division in fall or spring.
USES Culinary.
OTHER VARIETIES AND SPECIES
M. suavolens, *M. × villosa alopecuroides* Bowles' Mint.

Meum athamanticum
Spignel

Another name for this perennial herb is Baldmoney and it belongs to the parsnip family. The leaves are used in salads and other dishes as flavoring and the roots were formerly eaten as a vegetable. It is a popular herb in Scandinavian countries where it is called *bjørnerot*, or bear root and dedicated to the Norse god Balder, god of the summer sun. The flavor is slightly reminiscent of curry. Grown in a container it requires a good depth of soil although the roots will not reach their full depth for two or three years. It is an attractive plant and looks good in a container of herbs or in a rock garden.

HARDY (Zone 3).
HEIGHT AND SPREAD 12 in (30 cm) by 8 in (20 cm).
FLOWERS White or pink-tinged flowers carried in small heads.
FLOWERING Early summer.
FOLIAGE Light to mid-green leaves with finely cut edges like fennel.
SOIL Sandy loam. This plant will not tolerate alkaline soil.
SITE Sun or partial shade.
PROPAGATION Sow seeds *in situ* in spring and thin to 6 in (15 cm) apart. Divide mature plants in spring.
USES Culinary.
OTHER VARIETIES AND SPECIES None.

RIGHT *Sweet Cicely, an original "pot plant" was an ingredient in healing ointments and acts as a mild laxative.*

Monarda didyma
Bee Balm, Bergamot

A native perennial of North America, formerly used as a tea drunk by the Oswego Indians, bergamot was supposed to have antidepressant qualities and an infusion was used to treat colds. The plant is a good addition to any container or herbaceous border for it is attractive with deep red flowers that act as a focal point in any color scheme. It can be invasive and, if grown in a container, is best confined within a pot plunged in the soil. The flowers are much used in pot pourris because they are heavily scented with a strong citrus scent and their color is striking. As the name implies they are very attractive to bees.

HARDY (borderline) (Zones 4–6).
HEIGHT AND SPREAD 18–24 in (45–60 cm).
FLOWERS Scarlet ragged flowers with red tinged bracts (outer petals) held erect on stems.
FLOWERING Late summer.
FOLIAGE Dark, green, pointed, veined leaves. Some varieties have reddish veined leaves.
SOIL Fertile, moisture retentive.
SITE Sun or partial shade.
PROPAGATION By division in spring or fall.
USES Culinary (tea), pot pourri.
OTHER VARIETIES AND SPECIES
M. fistulosa (wild bergamot),
M. menthifolia, M. 'Cambridge Scarlet'.

Myrrhis odorata
Sweet Cicely

An attractive perennial herb with soft green fern-like leaves and pretty small white flowerheads like cow parsley, Sweet Cicely was one of the original "pot" herbs and was used in healing ointments for ulcers and as a tonic or gentle laxative. It was a sovereign remedy in cases of stomach trouble. However, if grown in a container you will need to replace the plant every two or three years as it forms a large clump and takes up considerable space. The leaves can be used in salads and to add sweetness to stewed fruit when wanted. The roots can also be cooked and eaten as a vegetable.

HARDY (Zone 3).
HEIGHT AND SPREAD 2–3 ft (60–90 cm) or more.
FLOWERS Small white star-shaped held in clusters in flat heads.
FLOWERING Early summer.
FOLIAGE Bright green fern-like leaves held on hairy stems.
SOIL Moist, well drained.
SITE Partial shade.
PROPAGATION Sow seed outside in fall or divide in spring.
USES Culinary, medicinal.
OTHER VARIETIES AND SPECIES None.

Nigella sativa
Love-in-a-Mist

A most attractive annual, a few plants can be raised in a container if you wish to brighten a group of herbs in midsummer. The most commonly grown nigella is *N. damascena* and its various hybrids, better known by the charming common name of Love-in-a-Mist. The thin slight leaves create a green mist in which the blue flowers appear framed. Also called fennel flower, *N. sativa* is no relation of fennel. It has white or paler blue flowers and is grown for the black aromatic nutmeg-flavored seeds used in curries as a substitute for pepper, and in baking. Another common name for the plant is nutmeg flower. In former times seeds were also used to treat indigestion.

HARDY ANNUAL (Zone 3).
HEIGHT AND SPREAD 18 in (45 cm) by 6 in (15 cm).
FLOWERS Pale blue, five-petalled flowers followed by attractive seedheads that are much used in flower arranging.
FLOWERING Summer.
FOLIAGE Gray-green, slight, pointed leaves like long needles.
SOIL Any, well-drained.
SITE Open and sunny.
PROPAGATION Sow seeds *in situ* in spring or fall. Some protection should be given for fall-sown varieties.
USES Culinary, medicinal, dried flower arrangements.
OTHER VARIETIES AND SPECIES
N. damascena, *N. hispanica*.

Ocimum basilicum
Sweet Basil

Basil is a favorite herb in the kitchen. The herb comes from tropical Asia and was brought to Europe from India in the 16th century. In temperate zones it should be grown in a trough on a hot sunny windowsill or outside in a container. When outside in the summer it requires frequent watering that is best carried out in the middle of the day. In sheltered gardens it can be grown in the vegetable garden although it dislikes strong winds. Its uses are extensive and favorite dishes that include basil are *Insalata tricolore* with tomatoes, basil and mozzarella cheese and *Soupe au Pistou*. There are a number of varieties with different-colored leaves from dark red to light green.

TENDER ANNUAL.
HEIGHT AND SPREAD 18 in (45 cm) by 12 in (30 cm).
FLOWERS Small white, pink-purple tinged, two-lipped carried on spikes.
FLOWERING Late summer.
FOLIAGE Intensely aromatic bright, shiny green leaves like small spinach.
SOIL Rich, well drained, moisture retentive..
SITE Sunny, sheltered.
PROPAGATION Sow seed at 55°F (13°C) in spring or *in situ* in summer.
USES Culinary.
OTHER VARIETIES AND SPECIES
O. basilicum 'Dark Opal' (purple leaves), *O. b.* 'Green Ruffles' (green ruffled leaves), *O. b.* 'Purple Ruffles' (purple ruffled leaves), *O. b.* var. *minimum* (Greek bush basil).

Origanum majorana
Sweet Marjoram

Origanum majorana, marjoram, is a member of the same genus as *O. vulgare*, oregano, and the plants are similar, botanically speaking. Both are favorite kitchen herbs but they come from different parts of the world and taste different. Marjoram comes from North Africa and South-West Asia although it is often found in South-West Europe on the Mediterranean coast. It has a sweet, rather floral scent. An evergreen subshrub it is usually grown as a tender perennial and needs to be brought in during the winter. It is an ideal herb for the container garden as it can be stood outside in the summer and brought inside for protection when frost threatens.

HALF-HARDY (Zones 7–9).
HEIGHT AND SPREAD 32 in (80 cm) by 18 in (45 cm).
FLOWERS Tubular pink or white flowers in panicles.
FLOWERING Summer.
FOLIAGE Soft, hairy, pointed, gray-green leaves.
SOIL Rich, well drained, fairly dry.
SITE Sun or partial shade.
PROPAGATION Sow seeds in spring at 50–55°C (10–13°C). Divide in spring or take basal cuttings in spring.
USES Culinary.
OTHER VARIETIES AND SPECIES
O. dictamnus (Cretan dittany), *O. microphyllum*, *O. rotundifolium*.

RIGHT *Love-in-a-Mist is a popular garden annual and an attractive container plant. It is closely related to love-in-a-mist.*

Origanum vulgare
Oregano

A favorite perennial Mediterranean herb used to flavor stews and many pasta dishes, oregano is a bushy perennial that carries many flowers on upright stalks. These are attractive to bees and insects and emerge pinkish-white from deep red bracts although there are a number of naturally occurring color variations. Many varieties have been bred for the herb garden among them , O. v. 'Aureum', gold leaves, 'Aureum Crispum', curly gold leaves, and 'Compactum', smaller in habit. 'Heiderose' is more upright and has pink flowers.

HARDY (Zone 5).
HEIGHT AND SPREAD 12–24 in (30–60 cm) by 8–12 in (20–30 cm).
FLOWERS Loose spikes of white to deep pink flowers carried in dense terminal clusters.
FLOWERING Late summer.
FOLIAGE Dark green to gold depending on the variety, round or pointed.
SOIL Rich, well drained to dry.
SITE Light shade.
PROPAGATION Division in spring, self-seeds.
USES Culinary.
OTHER VARIETIES AND SPECIES
O. onites (French marjoram),
O. hirtum (Greek marjoram).

Pelargonium
Scented Geranium

A number of pelargoniums have scented leaves and each one has its own distinctive perfume. In warm climates they can be grown out of doors as perennials but they are not frost-hardy and have to brought indoors in winter in cooler climates. They make attractive house plants. The leaves can be used to add flavor to sweets and in cakes and baking. The flowers and leaves can be dried and used in pot pourris.

HALF-HARDY (Zones 8–10).
HEIGHT AND SPREAD 8–24 in (20–60 cm) by 4–12 in (10–30 cm).
FLOWERS Summer.
FLOWERING White, mauve, pink or orange flowers held in clusters on stalks.
FOLIAGE Usually green, sometimes variegated, gold or silver, heart-shaped with deep lobes.
SOIL Light, well drained.
SITE Open, sunny.
PROPAGATION Take cuttings of non-flowering shoots in summer or spring.
USES Culinary, pot plants.
OTHER VARIETIES AND SPECIES
Scented-leaved pelargoniums include:
P. 'Aroma', P. 'Atomic Snowflake',
P. 'Clorinda', P. Fragrans Group,
P. 'Lilian Pottinger', P. 'Royal Oak'.

Pelargonium
'Graveolens'
Rose Geranium

The rose geranium is a vigorous evergreen perennial that is grown commercially for its oil. It has a strong lemony-rose scent and is used in the kitchen to flavor cakes and tea as well as in pot pourris and fingerbowls. There are a number of other rose-scented geraniums available.

HALF-HARDY (Zones 8–10).
HEIGHT AND SPREAD To 4 ft (1.2 m).
FLOWERS Small, pale pink held in dense clusters.
FLOWERING Summer.
FOLIAGE Mid-green, slightly rough, deeply lobed leaves.
SOIL Light, well drained.
SITE Sun.
PROPAGATION Take cuttings in spring and summer.
USES Culinary, pot pourri.
OTHER VARIETIES AND SPECIES
P. 'Attar of Roses', P. 'Lady Plymouth',
P. 'Rober's Lemon Rose'.

LEFT *Golden-leaved oregano is welcome in all containers because its foliage provides a high point in any color scheme.*

Perilla frutescens
Perilla

A colorful plant that adds a decorative feature to any container garden. It is used in the kitchen to flavor salads, soups and vegetables. The plant originally came from India and Japan where it is particularly popular. The green variety is used in the preparation of *sushi* and the purple form is used in pickling as it adds color to the preserve. The leaves are cinnamon-scented and carry a hint of curry.

TENDER ANNUAL.
HEIGHT AND SPREAD 1–2 ft (30–60 cm) by 9 in (23 cm).
FLOWERS Small tubular lavender to white flowers held on terminal spikes.
FLOWERING Late summer.
FOLIAGE Green or reddish purple depending on the variety grown. The aromatic leaves are long and nettle-like.
SOIL Rich, moisture retentive.
SITE Partial shade.
PROPAGATION Sow seeds in spring at 55–64°F (13–18°C).
USES Culinary.
OTHER VARIETIES AND SPECIES
P. frutescens var. *crispa*, *P. f. rubra*.

Petroselinum crispum
Parsley

Parsley is a biennial often grown as an annual. It is one of the best known herbs in the kitchen and is sprinkled over vegetables as a garnish and added to soups and stews. Parsley sauce is a traditional accompaniment for fish dishes. Parsley is rich in vitamin C and is used in the treatment of urinary disorders. It is difficult to germinate and requires a high temperature. Some people delay sowing until into the summer but it is a help to soak the seed in warm water overnight and pour boiling water down the seed drills if parsley is to be sown directly in the kitchen garden. It needs to be sown *in situ* as it resents being disturbed. It makes an excellent edge in a container of herbs. A number of varieties are available. The flat-leaved parsley or French parsley is hardier than the curly-leaved varieties and has a stronger flavor. *P. tuberosum*, turnip-rooted or Hamburg parsley has a large root that can be cooked or eaten raw.

FROST-HARDY (Zone 6).
HEIGHT AND SPREAD 12–24 in (30-60 cm) by 12 in (30 cm) depending on variety.
FLOWERS Insignificant greenish-yellow flowers carried in small flat heads in the second year.
FLOWERING Late summer.
FOLIAGE Rich, green, either curly or flat depending on the variety.
SOIL Fertile, moisture retentive.
SITE Sun, partial shade.
PROPAGATION Sow seed in summer at 60°F (15°C).
USES Culinary, medicinal.
OTHER VARIETIES AND SPECIES
P. crispum 'French', *P. c.* 'Greek',
P. c. var. *neapolitanum*, *P. c.* 'Afro',
P. c. 'Champion Moss Curled',
P. c. 'Moss Curled 2'.

ABOVE *The scented leaves of many pelargoniums are used in cakes, salads and pot pourris. They make good indoor plants.*

Portulaca oleracea
Wild Purslane

Most portalucas are semi-succulent trailing plants found in warm countries. *P. oleracea*, wild purslane, is a native of South Europe where it is grown as a hardy annual. The young succulent shoots are used in salads while the older shoots can be used as a pot herb for pickling. Given a warm sunny position it can be grown by the keen gardener who is interested in trying out-of-the-way salad vegetables.

TENDER ANNUAL.
HEIGHT AND SPREAD 6 in (15 cm) by 9 in (23 cm).
FLOWERS Small yellow flowers borne on the leaf axils.
FLOWERING Late summer.
FOLIAGE Fleshy, spatulate, green, red-tinged leaves.
SOIL Fertile, well drained.
SITE Full sun, sheltered.
PROPAGATION Sow seed at 55–64°F (13–18°C) in spring.
USES Culinary.
OTHER VARIETIES AND SPECIES
P. oleracea var. *aurea* (gold leaves).

LEFT *Primroses are one of the favorite flowers of spring. They do not flourish in full sun.*

Primula veris
Cowslip

A charming perennial wildflower that used to be more common than it is today, it can be planted in containers to add a homely touch in the spring. They are rather tricky to get started and the gardener may have to wait for a year or two before any plants germinate. In the right soil they establish themselves easily and once established they spread vigorously. The leaves were used in salads and the roots and flowers used medicinally. The flowers can also be picked to make cowslip wine.

HARDY (Zone 3).
HEIGHT AND SPREAD 4–12 in (10–30 cm) by 8 in (20 cm).
FLOWERS Deep yellow with orange red spots inside the flowers that are held in nodding heads inside a large green calyx, fragrant.
FLOWERING Late spring.
FOLIAGE Medium green, similar to the leaves of the primrose but not so spoon-shaped, downy on both sides.
SOIL Fertile, moisture retentive.
SITE Sun or partial shade. If grown in full sun the soil should not dry out.
PROPAGATION Sow seed in spring.
USES Culinary, formerly medicinal.
OTHER VARIETIES AND SPECIES
P. alpicola, P. elatior, P. palinuri, P. sikkimensis, P. veris hybrids.

Primula vulgaris
Primrose

The wild primrose is still a garden favorite with its pale yellow flowers with deeper yellow centers and delicate scent. Once established the plants can be divided and replanted every year to increase their number. They prefer rich soil and some shade and will not flourish in full sun. They are a charming plant for all positions in the garden and their flowers look good in containers where they can be inspected at close quarters. They are used in the same way as cowslips and the young leaves can be added to salads and the flowers candied and eaten.

HARDY (Zone 3).
HEIGHT AND SPREAD 8 in (20 cm).
FLOWERS Clusters of pale yellow five-petalled flowers with a deeper yellow center.
FLOWERING Early spring.
FOLIAGE Green, crinkly leaves with prominent veins forming a basal rosette.
SOIL Rich, fertile, moisture retentive.
SITE Shade or partial shade.
PROPAGATION Sow seed as soon as ripe, divide after flowering.
USES Culinary, formerly medicinal.
OTHER VARIETIES AND SPECIES
Many, some with double flowers.
P. vulgaris 'Alba Plena' (double white),
P. v. 'Double Sulphur' (double yellow),
P. v. ssp *sibthorpii* (pink, lilac, purple or white flowers).

Pycnanthemum pilosum
Mountain Mint

This attractive perennial can be grown in the container garden only if there is sufficient room because it takes up a good deal of space. One of its main attractions is that it flowers late in the summer and provides color and interest at a rather barren time of the year. It is much appreciated by the butterflies. The plant is a native of North America and will withstand dry conditions. Although its leaves are strongly peppermint scented it is not a true mint. However, the leaves can be used to make a peppermint-flavored tea.

HARDY (Zone 4).
HEIGHT AND SPREAD 2–3 ft (60–90 cm).
FLOWERS Lilac white spotted with purple carried on dense terminal clusters.
FLOWERING Late summer, fall.
FOLIAGE Light green, lance-shaped leaves held on radiating stalks.
SOIL Fertile, sandy loam.
SITE Sun or partial shade.
PROPAGATION Sow seeds in early spring, divide in spring, take tip cuttings in summer.
USES Culinary, bee and butterfly plant.
OTHER VARIETIES AND SPECIES
P. muticum, P. tenuifolium, P. virginiana.

Rosa rugosa
Hedgehog Rose, Japanese Rose

Roses can easily be grown in containers and many are suitable for training up walls and trellises. For the edible container garden the *Rosa rugosa* is a possible choice because the petals of the single pinkish-red fragrant flowers can be used in pot pourris and the flowers are followed by large tomato-shaped red to orange hips that can be used to make rose hip syrup, an excellent source of vitamin C. Roses are wonderful shrubs. Attar of roses is an ingredient in many soaps and perfumes and some roses such as *R. × centifolia* and *R. × damascena*, are used to produce essential oil.

HARDY (Zone 5).
HEIGHT AND SPREAD 3 ft (1 m) by 6 ft (1.8 m).
FLOWERS Cupped single pink to red flowers with yellow stamens.
FLOWERING Summer.
FOLIAGE Dark green wrinkled leaves.
SOIL Fertile, moisture retentive.
SITE Sun or partial shade.
PROPAGATION Take cuttings in the fall. Rose nurseries propagate by grafting and budding.
USES Culinary, pot pourri.
OTHER VARIETIES AND SPECIES
R. rugosa 'Alba' (white), *R. r. rubra* (purple-red), *R. gallica* var. *officinalis* (Apothecary's rose), *R. g.* 'Versicolor'.

Rosmarinus officinalis
Rosemary

Rosemary has been used in the home since Roman times and old herbals tell of the many properties of the plant. It is the herb of remembrance and friendship and is supposed to stimulate the mind. An evergreen shrub it can be grown easily in any container herb garden given a sheltered position. Although it comes from the Mediterranean it will tolerate some degree of frost. It flowers early in the year at the end of winter. In the kitchen it is the traditional accompaniment for roast lamb and can be used to flavor a number of other dishes. It is a slightly untidy plant, although some varieties are more compact than others but it will not regenerate from old wood so care must be taken when trimming it back.

FROST-HARDY (Zones 6–8).
HEIGHT AND SPREAD 3–6 ft (90–1.8 m) by 3 ft (90 cm) depending on the variety grown.
FLOWERS Short tubular, two-lipped, pale to dark blue, some varieties have white or pink flowers. The flowers appear all down the branches.
FLOWERING Winter to early spring.
FOLIAGE Dark green, hard, needle-like leaves with gray underneath. The leaves are very aromatic.
SOIL Well drained poor soil containing some lime.
SITE Sheltered and sunny.
PROPAGATION Take semi-ripe cuttings or layer in summer.
USES Culinary, formerly medicinal, cosmetics.
OTHER VARIETIES AND SPECIES
R. officinalis var. *albiflorus*,
R. o. 'Aureus', *R. o.* 'Benenden Blue',
R. o. 'Jackman's Prostrate',
R. o. 'Miss Jessopp's Upright',
R. o. Prostratus Group,
R. o. 'Sissinghurst Blue'.

LEFT *Rosemary grows well in containers and is hardier than might be supposed. It carries attractive blue flowers in early spring.*

Salvia officinalis
Common Sage

Salvias are a large group of plants including annuals, biennials, perennials and shrubs that are found in many gardens. Some are hardy, others that come from the tropics are greenhouse plants. The common sage, *Salvia officinalis*, and its varieties has been the best culinary herb for centuries and was formerly used in herbal medicine to treat depression, liver disorders, sore throats and mouth ulcers. An evergreen perennial or subshrub the leaves are often dried and stored for use and it is the main ingredient in sage and onion stuffing, a traditional accompaniment for roast poultry. It is also used to flavor fish, meat and cheese dishes.

HARDY/FROST-HARDY (Zones 4–8).
HEIGHT AND SPREAD 1–2 ft (30–60 cm) by 2 ft (60 cm).
FLOWERS Dark violet blue on long upright spikes.
FLOWERING Summer.
FOLIAGE Gray-green, oblong, rounded, woolly aromatic leaves.
SOIL Well drained, sandy loam.
SITE Open, sunny.
PROPAGATION Sow seeds in a cold frame in spring, take semi-ripe cuttings in summer.
USES Culinary, medicinal.
OTHER VARIETIES AND SPECIES
S. officinalis 'Albiflora',
S. o. broad-leaved, *S. o.* 'Icterina',
S. o. Purpurascens Group, *S. o.* 'Tricolor'.

Sanguisorba minor syn. *Poterium sanguisorba* Salad Burnet

A medieval "pot" herb much used in the kitchen to flavor soups, sauces and cheese, and whose leaves were also eaten raw in salads. Medicinally the leaves were dried and used as a tea to cure digestive disorders and to treat diarrhoea and haemorrhages. The roots, also used as a decoction for burns, make a black dye used in tanning. *P. sanguisorba* is a clump-forming perennial and if grown in a container has to be divided every two or three years to keep the plant within bounds. Herbaceous burnets such as *S. canadensis*, Canadian burnet, and *S. officinalis*, greater burnet, have large bottlebrush flowers on terminal spikes.

HARDY (Zone 3).
HEIGHT AND SPREAD 2 ft (60 cm).
FLOWERS Small red-brown petal-less flowers with globular heads.
FLOWERING Early summer.
FOLIAGE Gray-green pinnate leaves with rounded leaflets.
SOIL Poor, alkaline.
SITE Sunny.
PROPAGATION Sow seed *in situ* in spring. Divide in spring.
USES Culinary.
OTHER VARIETIES AND SPECIES
S. albiflora, *S. canadensis*, *S. obtusa*.

Satureja hortensis Summer Savory

There are two sorts of savory. Winter savory is a foliage plant ideal for a low-growing container that is often used to flavor beans. Summer savory is an annual, that can be grown to fill any bare areas. Sow seed *in situ* in spring. The hairy erect stems have small white flowers on spikes in the summer. If they are grown for use in the kitchen the plants should be pulled up and allowed to dry naturally and then the leaves should be picked off and stored. The flavor is slightly reminiscent of thyme and it can be used sparingly in a number of meat dishes and stuffings. A tea made from the leaves acts as a tonic and flowering shoots in clothes will repel moths.

HARDY ANNUAL.
HEIGHT AND SPREAD 12 in (30 cm).
FLOWERS White to pink held in spikes on the leaf axils.
FLOWERING Late summer.
FOLIAGE Long, dark green, leathery pointed leaves.
SOIL Well drained, sandy loam.
SITE Sunny.
PROPAGATION Sow seeds *in situ* in spring when the soil has warmed up.
USES Culinary, formerly medicinal.
OTHER VARIETIES AND SPECIES
S. coerulea, *S. montana* (winter savory), *S. m.* prostrate white, *S. spicigera*.

Silybum marianum Milk Thistle

Although a fairly large thistle might not be the first choice of plant for the container, the milk thistle is a fine foliage plant and will provide a talking point for any gardener. The other common names for the plant are Blessed or Holy Thistle and St Mary's Thistle; the legend has it that the milky veins running on the leaves of the plant were caused by the milk of the Virgin Mary falling onto them when the infant Jesus was being fed. The plant is a biennial and does not flower until the second year when the purple-pink flowers can be trimmed and cooked as a vegetable like artichokes. The stems and leaves can also be trimmed, cooked and eaten and the roots can be boiled like parsnips. Medicinally it was used to aid digestion and as a cure for travel sickness.

HARDY (Zone 5).
HEIGHT AND SPREAD 5 ft (1.5 m) by 3 ft (90 cm).
FLOWERS Purple-pink fragrant flowers surrounded by thistly spikes.
FLOWERING Summer.
FOLIAGE Spiny shiny green leaves with prominent white veins.
SOIL Well drained.
SITE Open, sunny.
PROPAGATION Sow seeds *in situ* in spring or early summer. Thin out unwanted plants.
USES Culinary, formerly medicinal.
OTHER VARIETIES AND SPECIES
None.

LEFT *The milk thistle is a striking plant and the flowers can be cooked and eaten like artichokes. The plant is biennial.*

LEFT *A good-size clump of betony looks superb in full bloom.*

Tagetes patula
French Marigold

French marigolds are well worth planting in containers as well as borders and in vegetable gardens as companion plants. They deter whitefly, carrot fly and imported cabbage moths. They are pleasantly scented and decorative and the flowerheads can be picked and dried and used in pot pourris. The leaves of *T. lucida* (mint marigold) taste of tarragon and can be used to make a flavored tea. Marigolds are divided into four main groups: African marigolds, French marigolds, Afro-French marigolds and Signet marigolds according to the habit and flower color. Each has different flower shapes.

CAUTION The leaves of all tagetes may cause skin allergies.

TENDER ANNUAL.
HEIGHT AND SPREAD 12 in (30 cm).
FLOWERS Yellow, orange or bronze with five petals.
FLOWERING Summer.
FOLIAGE Dark green deeply divided aromatic leaves.
SOIL Well drained, poorish.
SITE Open, sunny.
PROPAGATION Sow seed *in situ* in late spring.
USES Companion plant, pot pourri.
OTHER VARIETIES AND SPECIES
T. lemmonii, *T. lucida*, *T.* Aurora Series, *T.* Bonanza Series, *T.* Safari Series.

Smyrnium olusatrum
Black Lovage

Another large biennial herb suitable for large containers, Alexanders, or black lovage, was formerly used as a vegetable before celery became popular. It has a pronounced celery taste and the leaves, stems, stalks and flowers are all used in salads and stews, or cooked as a vegetable after blanching. One of the best ways to grow it in containers is as an annual leaf crop. The species *S. perfoliatum* is grown for its cut flowers.

FROST-HARDY (Zones 5–7).
HEIGHT AND SPREAD 3 ft (90 cm) by 2 ft (60 cm).
FLOWERS Small yellow-green flowers held in small heads.
FLOWERING Midsummer.
FOLIAGE Large, shiny, dark green leaves divided into several leaflets.
SOIL Dry, well drained.
SITE Open, sunny.
PROPAGATION Sow seed *in situ* in spring.
USES Culinary.
OTHER VARIETIES AND SPECIES
S. perfoliatum.

Stachys officinalis
Betony

An ancient perennial medicinal herb, wood betony or woundwort, was supposed to possess magical healing properties and was also used to ward off evil spirits. It was common in herb gardens and churchyards in the Middle Ages. It is an attractive plant with upright pink or purple flowers. The leaves can be dried and used to make a herbal tea that is mildly sedative or used in herbal cigarettes.

HARDY (Zone 4).
HEIGHT AND SPREAD 1–2 ft (30–60 cm) by 1 ft (30 cm).
FLOWERS Upright stems of dense white to purple, mainly pink flowers.
FLOWERING Summer.
FOLIAGE Mid-green, oblong rough, toothed leaves.
SOIL Sandy loam, but will tolerate most soil conditions.
SITE Partial shade.
PROPAGATION Sow seeds in a cold frame in spring. Divide plants in spring.
USES Medicinal, tea.
OTHER VARIETIES AND SPECIES
S. byzantina, *S. macrantha*, *S. officinalis* 'Alba', *S. o.* 'Rosea Superba'.

Tanacetum parthenium
Feverfew

As its name implies, feverfew has long been used in medicine as a tonic to reduce fever and treat indigestion. It is now available in tablet form and is used in the treatment of migraine and arthritis. The leaves are sometimes made into a poultice for sprains and the dried leaves can also be used in the home to repel moths. The plant is a perennial. It has a pungent smell and the leaves are bitter to taste.

CAUTION The leaves may cause mouth ulcers and the plant should not be taken during pregnancy.

HARDY (Zone 5).
HEIGHT AND SPREAD 2 ft (60 cm) by 18 in (45 cm).
FLOWERS Small white daisylike with yellow centers in clusters.
FLOWERING Summer.
FOLIAGE Yellow-green scalloped leaves on prominent stalks.
SOIL Any, well drained.
SITE Sun or partial shade.
PROPAGATION Sow seed at 50–55°F (10–13°C) in early spring. Divide in spring.
USES Medicinal, moth repellent.
OTHER VARIETIES AND SPECIES
T. parthenium 'Aureum', *T. p.* 'Rowallane', *T. vulgare*.

Tanacetum vulgare
Tansy

Tansy cakes and puddings were traditionally eaten at Easter time and the herb was also valued in medicine as a tonic, a febrifuge – for removing fever, and vermifuge – for expelling worms from animals. It was also used as an insecticide. This perennial herb can be grown in containers but it dislikes wet soil so it should be watered sparingly. It will form a clump that may have to be replaced after a year or two.

HARDY (Zone 4).
HEIGHT AND SPREAD 2 ft (60 cm).
FLOWERS Button-shaped bright yellow held on terminal flat heads.
FLOWERING Late summer.
FOLIAGE Dark green fernlike with lance-shaped toothed leaflets.
SOIL Well drained, fertile.
SITE Sun or partial shade.
PROPAGATION Division in spring or autumn. Sow seed in spring at 50–55°F (10–13°C).
USES Medicinal, culinary.
OTHER VARIETIES AND SPECIES
T. vulgare var. *crispum*, *T. v.* 'Isla Gold', *T. v.* 'Silver Lace'.

Thymus vulgaris
Common Thyme

A well-known and important herb, common thyme is a perennial subshrub and is still used in the kitchen after many centuries to flavor meat, fish and vegetable dishes, and in bouquets garni. It is a charming, attractive plant for the herb container. A number of thymes can be used in the kitchen including *T. herba-barona*, with the scent of caraway, traditionally used to flavor a baron of beef, and some creeping thymes. Thyme is also used as an antiseptic and an insect repellent.

FROST-HARDY (borderline) (Zones 5–9).
HEIGHT AND SPREAD 12 in (30 cm).
FLOWERS Small white to purple flowers in dense or loose terminal clusters.
FLOWERING Summer.
FOLIAGE Gray-green, linear to elliptic leaves with pale underside.
SOIL Well drained, sandy loam.
SITE Open, sunny.
PROPAGATION Sow seeds in spring in a cold frame. Take semi-ripe cuttings in summer.
USES Culinary, medicinal.
OTHER VARIETIES AND SPECIES
T. pulegioides, *T. herba-barona*, *T. × citriodora* 'Aureus', *T. × c.* 'Bertram Anderson', *T. v. aureus* 'Silver Posie'.

LEFT *Feverfew has attractive, white daisy-like flowers. An infusion is good for migraines and arthritis.*

LEFT *Johnny-jump-ups are grown as an annual and bear scented flowers from spring to fall. The flowers taste peppery and are good in salads.*

Tropaeolum majus
Nasturtium

The common nasturtium is a good annual climber to add to the herb container. It can be allowed to fall over the front or grown at the back as a climber up a wall or trellis. The leaves and flowers can both be eaten although the flowers are more often used as a garnish. Both have a hot, rather peppery, flavor. The seeds are followed by spherical fruits that contain three seeds. These and the young flowers can be pickled. Medicinally the herb was used as a digestive and to cure urinary disorders; the seeds were used in poultices to heal boils and sores.

TENDER ANNUAL (Zones 8–10), perennial in warm climates.
HEIGHT AND SPREAD 3–5 ft (90–1.5 m) by 6–10 ft (1.8–3 m) or more.
FLOWERS Long-spurred red, orange and yellow.
FLOWERING Late summer.
FOLIAGE Green, wavy, kidney-shaped leaves held on stalks.
SOIL Moist, well drained. The plants flower best on poorer soils.
SITE Sun or partial shade.
PROPAGATION Sow seed *in situ* in late spring or earlier at 55–61°F (13–16°C).
USES Culinary, medicinal.
OTHER VARIETIES AND SPECIES
T. majus 'Alaska', *T. m.* 'Hermine Grashoff', *T. m.* 'Red Wonder', *T. speciosum*, *T. tricolorum*, *T. tuberosum*.

Viola odorata
Sweet Violet

A well-known sweet-smelling perennial flower of spring that flourishes in wild gardens and is a welcome plant in any container provided it can be be grown in semi-shade in moist soil. Violets were valued in medicine in the treatment of bronchial disorders and is also used to alleviate bruising and as a mild sedative. The flowers are also used in perfumes and cosmetics and they can also be candied or used to flavor meat dishes.

HARDY (Zones 4–6).
HEIGHT AND SPREAD 4 in (15 cm) spreading.
FLOWERS White or violet, five-petalled, small, fragrant.
FLOWERING Early spring.
FOLIAGE Dark green, glossy oval leaves held on short stalks.
SOIL Moisture retentive, fertile.
SITE Shade or partial shade.
PROPAGATION Sow seeds in fall, divide in late winter or early spring.
USES Culinary, perfume, medicinal.
OTHER VARIETIES AND SPECIES
V. odorata 'Alba', *V. o.* 'Alba Plena', *V. o. rosea*, *V. o.* 'Wellsiana'.

Viola tricolor
Wild Pansy, Heartsease

A delightful small flower for the container gardener because it can be planted around the edges of the containers to provide long-lasting color and interest. The flowers are edible and are sometimes sprinkled on salads to provide decoration. The plant formerly was used medicinally as a blood purifier, a tonic, and to reduce blood pressure; it was also used to treat ulcers, sores and various skin conditions.

HARDY ANNUAL or short-lived perennial.
HEIGHT AND SPREAD 8 in (20 cm).
FLOWERS Three-colored; deep violet, pale lilac purple, yellow tinged with white. The flowers are scented and the dark petals frame the three lighter lower ones.
FLOWERING All summer.
FOLIAGE Dark green toothed, lance-shaped with three leaflets.
SOIL Fertile sandy loam.
SITE Open, sunny.
PROPAGATION Sow seed in spring in containers in a cold frame. Take tip cuttings in summer if wanted. The plant self-seeds freely.
USES Medicinal, culinary.
OTHER VARIETIES AND SPECIES
V. 'Bowles Black', *V.* 'Johnny Jump Up', *V.* 'Prince Henry'.

Herb Recipes

Teas

The principle for making herbal teas is the same for all herbs. The main herbal teas, all of which are considered to have medicinal properties, are: sage, aromatic and astringent; mint, digestive and anti-spasmodic; pennyroyal, a tonic; tansy, for colic and gout; fennel leaves, for kidney complaints; dillwater, for wind; marigold flowers, for the liver; hyssop, for catarrh and chest complaints; rosemary, for headaches; lemon balm, for fevers.

Calendulas

Chamomile tea

1 Pick some chamomile flowers and dry them.

2 To make this classic herbal tea, allow 1 tsp of dried flowers for a pint of boiling water.

3 Allow the flowerheads to infuse for 5 minutes. Add sugar to sweeten if you wish.

Peppermint tea sorbet

INGREDIENTS

scant 2 cups (450 ml, ¾ pt,) water
½ oz (15 g) peppermint tea leaves
4 fl oz (125 ml) sugar syrup – made by boiling 2 lb (900 g) superfine sugar with 4 cups (1½ pt, 900 ml) water and simmering for 10 minutes. This can be stored for 2–3 weeks.
Serves 4–6

1 Boil the water in a saucepan and add the peppermint tea leaves.

2 Leave covered for about 3 hours. Strain through a nylon sieve.

3 Mix the tea and sugar syrup together and freeze in an icecream maker. If you haven't got an icecream maker, put the mixture into trays in the freezer. Freeze until it has formed into a slush.

4 Remove and put the slush in a blender for 1 minute. Refreeze until hard.

Mint

Dandelion tea

1 Pick 5–6 leaves from a young dandelion plant. Tear the leaves into strips.

2 Place the leaves in a mug and then fill with boiling water. Infuse for 5–10 minutes.

3 Remove the leaves and add sugar to taste. Dandelion is a mild laxative and dandelion tea should not be drunk in large quantities.

Salads
Dandelion salad
Dandelions (pissenlits) are grown in France for eating. To make a simple salad:

INGREDIENTS
½ lb (225 g) young dandelion leaves
3–4 strips of streaky bacon
3 tbsp red wine vinegar
Serves 4–6

1 Wash the dandelion leaves and shake them dry.

2 Fry the bacon, chop into small pieces and scatter on the dandelion leaves.

3 Add the red wine vinegar to the bacon fat, heat until it begins to bubble and mix it with the remains in the pan. Pour this over the leaves. Eat while warm.

Herb and flower salad

Nasturtium

INGREDIENTS
1 round or salad bowl lettuce
8 sprigs of chervil
Nasturtium flowers
Serves 4–6

1 Combine the lettuce leaves and chervil. Add half the nasturtium flowers.

2 Dress with a light vinaigrette and scatter the remaining flowers over the salad as a garnish.

Sauces
Sauce verte

INGREDIENTS

1 cup (300 ml, ½ pt) thick mayonnaise
2 oz (60 g) herbs – the leaves of young spinach, watercress, parsley, chives, tarragon, chervil.

Allow 2 parts spinach and watercress to one each of the others.

1 Bring a saucepan of water to the boil and put all the leaves in the boiling water for 3–4 minutes.

2 Drain and dry the leaves, then purée them in a food processor. Traditionally they were pounded and passed through a fine sieve.

3 Add the purée to the mayonnaise just before serving.

Chervil

Parsley sauce

The easiest parsley sauce is made by adding a good handful of finely chopped parsley to 1 cup (300 ml, ½ pt) béchamel sauce. Here is a richer version usually served with ham.

INGREDIENTS
1 oz (30 g) butter
½ oz (15 g) plain flour
½ pt (300 ml) liquid from the cooked ham
1 egg yolk
Lemon juice
2 tbsp single cream
1 tbsp chopped parsley

1 Melt half the butter and flour together in a pan, add the ham liquid and stir until the sauce thickens.

2 Combine the egg yolk, lemon juice and cream in a bowl. Pour a little of the hot sauce into the bowl, stir together and then return the mixture to the sauce.

3 Stir very gently over a low heat for 2–3 minutes. Do not allow the sauce to boil.

4 Remove from the heat. Add the chopped parsley and the remainder of the butter cut into small pieces.

ALTERNATIVE

A simple herb sauce can be made by making a thin well-flavored béchamel sauce and then adding the finely chopped leaves of parsley, tarragon, chervil and chives. Use 2 tbsp of chopped herbs for every pint (600 ml) of sauce.

Desserts
Mint cup

INGREDIENTS
2 sprigs of fresh mint
½ tsp sugar
Cracked ice
½ tsp lemon juice
2 tbsp grapefruit juice
Soda or tonic water as preferred
Borage

1 Crush the mint and place with the sugar in a tall glass. Fill the glass with cracked ice.

2 Add the lemon and grapefruit juice, fill the glass with tonic or soda water and stir until the glass is frosted.

3 Decorate with flowering sprigs of borage.

Rose cream tart

INGREDIENTS
1 egg
10–12 petals of a red or pink rose
Superfine sugar
8 oz (225 g) flaky pastry
½ cup (150 ml, ¼ pt) plain yogurt
1¼ cup (300 ml 1¼ cup) whipping cream
2 tbsp rosewater
Serves 4–6

1 Whip the egg white until stiff. Coat each petal with egg white and superfine sugar. Dry in a cool oven 230°F (110°C, Gas Mark 1) for about 1 hour.

2 Roll out the pastry into a ¼ in (5 mm) thick, 10 in (25 cm) circle. Bake the pasty at 400°F (200°C, Gas Mark 6) for 25 minutes. Let the pastry cool completely.

3 Whip the cream stiffly. Fold in the yogurt, egg yolk and 2 tbsp superfine sugar. Whisk in the rosewater. Spoon over the pastry base, decorate with the petals and serve immediately.

Dog rose

Herbal beauty treatments

Herbs have long been used for cosmetic preparations. Here are a selection of recipes that you can try at home.

Chamomile and bran face mask

INGREDIENTS
1 tsp dried chamomile flowers
2 tbsp bran
1 tsp acacia (or clear) honey
¾ cup (175 ml, 6 fl oz) boiling water

1 Put the chamomile flowers in a bowl and pour the water over them. Let it cool for 30 minutes or so.

2 Mix the bran with the honey and then add 3 tbsp of the chamomile liquid. Apply the mixture as a face mask, avoiding the eyes.

3 Leave the mask in place for 10 minutes. Rinse off with warm water. It softens the skin, leaving it fresh, smooth and clear.

Fennel cleanser

INGREDIENTS
1 tbsp fennel seeds
1 cup (225 ml, 8 fl oz) boiling water
1 tsp acacia (or clear) honey
2 tbsp skimmed milk

1 Crush the fennel seeds in a bowl and then add the boiling water. Allow to infuse for 30 minutes or so.

2 When the water has cooled, strain it into another bowl, add the honey and milk. Stir together.

3 Funnel the liquid into a bottle and keep in the refrigerator for use as a skin cleanser.

Lemon verbena hair rinse
There are a number of herbal tonics that can be applied to the hair as stimulants. This is one of the best scented.

INGREDIENTS
1 handful of lemon verbena leaves
1 cup (225 ml, 8 fl oz) boiling water

1 Strip the lemon verbena leaves from the stalks and place them in a bowl. Pour over the boiling water and let it stand for at least 1 hour.

2 Strain, bottle and then use as a hair rinse after conditioning.

Herbal scents and flavorings

Herb and hop pillows

Hops and other herbs believed to have sleep-inducing properties were traditionally used to scent pillows and promote a good night's rest.

The exact proportions of herbs for a herbal pillow or cushion can be varied but a good mixture to try is 1 part each of mint, lavender, lemon verbena and rosemary leaves to 3 parts lemon-scented geranium leaves, all dried. Pick the herbs and flowers before they are fully open on a dry, sunny day and hang them up to dry in a cool airy room. When they are quite dry they can be stripped from their stalks and used for pillows or sachets. Mix the leaves together and put into individual sachets, and then place the sachets inside pillows or cushions.

Pot pourris

A mixture of herbs and flowers with fragrant oil looks attractive and will fill a room with its delicious fragrance.

Good flowers for a pot pourri include scented roses, carnations, lavender, orange, heliotrope, rosemary, violets, woodruff and honeysuckle. Scented leaves include marjoram, sweet balm, lemon verbena, rosemary and pennyroyal. Deep red roses and the blue flowers of borage are particularly welcome for the splash of color they provide, and lemon and orange rind can also be added.

Pick the flowers and leaves in a dry period when there has been no rain for 24 hours and the morning dew has vanished. Leave them to dry, preferably on a wire rack in an airy room.

Before mixing the ingredients for the pot pourri, make sure that they are all thoroughly dry and no vestige of moisture remains, otherwise the mixture will mold.

Sweet pot pourri

INGREDIENTS

4 good handfuls of dried leaves and flowers. If you wish, this pot pourri can be made with dried herbs only.
10 slices dried orange
6 cinnamon sticks
4 nutmegs
1 tsp mint essential oil
1 tbsp sweet orange essential oil
1 tbsp orris root
China or glass bowl

1 Mix all the ingredients together except for the orris root.

2 When the oils have been absorbed, tip the mixture into a plastic bag, add the orris root, and seal.

3 Leave to mature for a week or two, shaking the bag from time to time. Tip the mixture into the bowl.

Hops

Vegetables

Vegetables grown in containers can be picked fresh and eaten immediately; they taste better than any vegetable you can buy. You know exactly how they have been grown and the fertilizers that have been used, so they can be raised as genuinely organic crops. You also have the satisfaction of producing your own food.

Containers devoted to vegetables need very careful planning. Plant vegetables closer together than is recommended on the seed packets and grow quick-maturing crops, such as lettuces, beside those that take longer to reach maturity. Try to grow those that will give you the greatest yields in the smallest space.

Plan the vegetables to display contrasting colors of foliage and form. Also consider how the vegetables look as they mature. Onions, for instance, look straggly and floppy as they ripen and a worn-out broccoli plant is not a thing of beauty. If you can, conceal the containers of these vegetables in a corner until you can harvest them and replant.

(NOTE Soil preferences are given for plants grown in open ground. For container gardeners this provides an indication of the type and richness of the most suitable compost and growing conditions for that plant.)

Allium cepa
Onion

Onions are a less popular choice for containers than spring onions or shallots, because they are untidy and straggly in growth. As with all vegetables, however, onions grown and picked from your own garden taste much better than anything you can buy in a supermarket. Onions can be grown in two ways: by sowing seed or planting sets, specially grown small bulbs. It is easiest to plant sets, particularly if you have limited room in a container.

SOW Plant sets in late winter or early spring. Sow seed in cells in winter at 50–60°F (10–16°C), harden off in spring and plant out in late spring when the plants have two true leaves.
PLANTING DEPTH Push sets into the soil so that the bulb tips are just showing.
PLANTING DISTANCE Thin seed-raised onions and plant sets 2 in (5 cm) apart.
SOIL Fertile, well drained.
SITE Open, sunny.
HARVEST Onions can be pulled and used fresh at any time. To store, let the foliage die down naturally and then lift the onions carefully and let the foliage and skins dry off completely. Onions with thick necks should be used first.
USES Used in almost all soups and stews as a flavoring. Can be chopped or sliced and fried, used as the main ingredient in onion sauce or onion tart, or boiled whole.
OTHER VARIETIES 'Stuttgarter Giant', 'Ailsa Craig', 'Sturon', 'Rijnsburger'.
RED-SKINNED VARIETIES 'Red Baron'.

Allium cepa
Aggregatum Group
Spring Onions

Spring onions are used in salads and are easy to grow during the summer. With their dark green upright leaves, they make an attractive fringe in a container and can also be used to flavor light summer soups.

SOW Seed in rows from late winter (in mild areas) through to early summer
PLANTING DEPTH ½ in (1 cm).
PLANTING DISTANCE If you have room, plant rows 4 in (10 cm) apart.
SOIL Fertile, well drained.
SITE Open, sunny.
HARVEST Pull onions when they have reached maturity. Spring onions will be ready in about 22 weeks.
USES Salads, summer soups.
OTHER VARIETIES 'White Lisbon', 'North Holland Blood Red'.

RIGHT *Beets are an excellent vegetable and should be picked and eaten young. They can be stored over the winter in dry sand or peat.*

LEFT *Swiss chard is an
excellent vegetable that lasts
a long time. It prefers growing
in some shade.*

Beta vulgaris
Beets

Beets are frequently pickled in vinegar, but
cooked fresh and served with butter and
garlic they are a culinary delight. The decorative leaves are edible and beets grown in a
container look attractive in a patio garden.

SOW Outdoors when the soil has warmed
up, from mid-spring till midsummer. Soak
the seed overnight before sowing. The seed
will germinate in 10–14 days.
PLANTING DEPTH 1 in (2.5 cm).
PLANTING DISTANCE Sow two seeds
every 4 in (10 cm). Remove one plant if
both germinate.
SOIL Fertile, well drained. Add slow
release fertilizer to the container 2–3 weeks
before sowing.
SITE Open, sunny.
HARVEST Pull beets from midsummer
onwards. Small beets are the most tender.
If grown for storage over winter, lift in
early fall, twist off the foliage by hand and
store in layers in dry peat.
USES Kitchen vegetable. The main
ingredient in *borscht*, a traditional Russian
and Polish soup.
OTHER VARIETIES 'Chioggia', 'Burpees
Golden', 'Detroit'.

Beta vulgaris
Cicla Group,
Perpetual Beet

Perpetual beet is a close relation of beets
and Swiss chard that can become perennial
in Zone 7 south. It has large long leaves,
glossy and rounded at the top. It is easy to
grow and can be grown in a small space in
a container or growbag, where it should be
given a liquid fertilizer every two or three
weeks. It can also grow quite well in places
that receive little sun, unlike most vegetables. Seed sown in the spring will provide
leaves right through the fall, provided that
the crop is regularly picked. The young
leaves have the most tender flavor. In the
kitchen, perpetual beet is an excellent alternative to spinach, although it does not have
quite the same refinement of flavor, and
should be cooked in the same way.

SOW Sow mid-spring. The seeds take
10–14 days to germinate.
PLANTING DEPTH 1 in (2.5 cm).
PLANTING DISTANCE 3–4 in (7.5–10
cm) apart. Thin to 6–8 in (15–20 cm)
apart.
SOIL Any fertile, well manured soil. If the
soil is acid, lime should be applied in winter before sowing.
SITE Grows best in sun or light shade.
HARVEST Midsummer onwards. Given
some protection, leaves can be harvested
throughout the winter.
USES Kitchen vegetable, good in soups
and soufflés. Can be frozen.
OTHER VARIETIES Seldom listed.

Beta vulgaris
Cicla Group
Swiss Chard, Silver
Chard, Ruby Chard

One of the best vegetables to grow in a container or growbag on a patio, Swiss chard
has striking, brilliant red stems and red-
veined green leaves while silver chard has
broad white stalks and white-ribbed green
leaves. They are members of the same group
as beets and grow under the same conditions. Their habit is slightly different, for
the chards have thicker and longer stems
and can be harvested a few leaves at a time.
They have a pronounced spinach flavor.
They can be picked young and cooked as
spinach, or left for longer in the ground
when the stalks, which have some of the flavor of asparagus, can be cut off and cooked
separately. Ruby chard looks more striking
than silver chard but the latter has a better
flavor and thicker stalks.

SOW Spring.
PLANTING DEPTH 1 in (2.5 cm).
PLANTING DISTANCE 3–4 in (7.5–10
cm) apart. Thin to 6–8 in (15–20 cm)
apart.
SOIL Any fertile, well manured soil. If the
soil is acid, lime should be applied in win-
ter before sowing.
SITE Grows best in sun or light shade.
HARVEST Midsummer onwards.
USES Dual-purpose kitchen vegetable. The
stalks and leaves can be cooked and eaten
separately.
OTHER VARIETIES 'Ruby Chard', 'Bright
Lights'.
SWISS (SILVER) CHARD 'Fordhook
Giant', 'Lyon', 'Lucullus'.

Brassica juncea
Mustard Greens

Mustard greens are one of a large group of vegetables, the Oriental brassicas, that are becoming increasingly popular. They are quick-maturing and most of them have a spicy flavor. Mustard greens often have attractive purple leaves that look good in a container garden but grow more slowly than some of the other Oriental greens. While they can be eaten raw in salads, they are generally cooked, either steamed or used in a stir-fry. Tatsoi, *Brassica rapa*, is another fast-maturing crop that can be grown in the same way. It should be sown in spring or late summer.

SOW Midsummer.
PLANTING DEPTH ¹/₂ in (1 cm).
PLANTING DISTANCE Scatter seed thinly and thin to 6 in (15 cm) apart or more if there is space available.
SOIL Fertile, well drained. Do not let the medium dry out.
SITE Sun or partial shade.
HARVEST Fall and winter. Plants mature between 6–13 weeks.
USES Can be used in salads when young or cooked as a vegetable.
OTHER VARIETIES 'Southern Giant', 'Green Wave', 'Osaka Purple'.

Brassica oleracea
Acephala Group
Kale

Picked young and cooked with care, kale, or borecole, can be a splendid vegetable. It is the hardiest of winter vegetables. In many areas, it provides fresh greens in the depth of winter. It is generally served with bacon or pork dishes. Ornamental kales provide color over the fall, and the leaves can be used as a garnish for fall salads. The best varieties for containers are the dwarf forms of curly kale, which reach about 12 in (30 cm) in height. The leaves are frilly and look like large parsley.

SOW Seed thinly in containers or pots in early summer.
PLANTING DEPTH ¹/₂ in (1 cm).
PLANTING DISTANCE Thin out seedlings to 3 in (7.5 cm) apart and then plant out when the plants have reached 4 in (10 cm) high, allowing 12 in (30 cm) or more between plants depending on the space available.
SOIL Ordinary garden soil or potting compost; apply a little fertilizer before planting.
SITE Sun, partial shade.
HARVEST Start harvesting in early winter, taking a few young shoots from the crown of each plant.
USES Kitchen vegetable. Can be frozen.
OTHER VARIETIES 'Winterbor', 'Toscano', 'Red Russian', a variety with reddish leaves.

Brassica oleracea
Botrytis Group
Cauliflower

Cauliflowers are probably the most difficult of all brassicas to grow properly; they require time and care. They need a regular supply of water throughout their growing period and too often this clashes with absences from the home during summer holidays. Checks in growth result in small, deformed heads. An automatic watering system can overcome this. In warm spots, cauliflowers can be grown so that they are available throughout the year. The easiest to grow are the summer and fall varieties; true winter cauliflowers are only half-hardy. There are some excellent mini-varieties now available which are well suited to container gardens.

SOW
SUMMER VARIETIES Sow seed in midwinter under glass.
FALL VARIETIES. Sow seed outdoors from mid-spring onwards. Sow all seeds thinly in containers or pots.
PLANTING DEPTH ¹/₂ in (1 cm).
PLANTING DISTANCE Thin out seedlings to 3 in (7.5 cm) apart and then plant out when the plants have reached 4 in (10 cm) high. Allow at least 18 in (45 cm) between plants, or 6 in (15 cm) for mini-cauliflowers.
SOIL Fertile, moisture retentive. Apply fertilizer before planting.
SITE Partial shade.
HARVEST
SUMMER VARIETIES Midsummer to early autumn. Mini-cauliflowers are ready after 13–18 weeks.
FALL VARIETIES Late fall. Pick and eat or freeze all cauliflowers as they become ready. They will not keep in the ground and the heads will deteriorate.
USES Kitchen vegetable, crudités. Young cauliflowers should be cooked carefully, they are easy to overcook.
OTHER VARIETIES
SUMMER 'Snow Crown',
MIDSEASON 'Amazing'.
PURPLE 'Violet Queen'.

RIGHT 'Dwarf Green Curled' kale which is most suitable for growing in a container as a winter vegetable.

Brassica oleracea
Capitata Group
Cabbage

A cabbage might not be everyone's choice for the limited space available in a container garden but they are considerably more compact than most brassicas and a number of the red and savoy cabbages are attractive plants for a patio garden. Most cabbages are grown to mature in the fall but spring cabbages are also a possibility for the keen gardener and provide fresh vegetables in the first months of the year.

SOW Summer/fall/winter cabbages thinly in succession between early spring and early summer. In warm areas, sow spring cabbages in late summer.
PLANTING DEPTH ½ in (1 cm).
PLANTING DISTANCE Thin out seedlings to 3 in (7.5 cm) apart and plant out when the plants have 5 or 6 leaves.
SOIL Fertile, well drained, moisture retaining. Cabbages like firm soil. Apply a general fertilizer before planting. Protect young plants from birds.
SITE Open, sun or partial shade.
HARVEST From early fall onwards. Red and savoy cabbages can be left in the ground for several weeks without harm.
USES Well-known kitchen vegetable. Savoy cabbage is a favorite culinary variety and red cabbage is usually cooked slowly with onions, bacon, apples and spices.
OTHER VARIETIES 'Dynamo' (mini), 'Primax', 'Tendersweet' (all seasons) 'Kilosa' (savoy), 'Red Express' (red).

RIGHT Purple sprouting broccoli is probably the best winter vegetable to grow for eating in early spring. Pick the spears regularly.

Brassica oleracea
Gongylodes Group
Kohlrabi

Kohlrabi is an odd looking vegetable which tastes rather like cauliflower, is very nutritious and can either be cooked or grated and eaten raw in salads. It is a slightly unusual looking bulb with a few leaves emerging at random from a globe on long stalks. Both white and purple kohlrabi are available and it is best to grow the modern varieties for they remain sweeter and more tender than the old fashioned forms that were best eaten when they were small, the size of a tennis ball. Kohlrabi is a quick-maturing vegetable and can be sown in succession throughout the year.

SOW *In situ* from spring to late summer, or sow in trays and transplant.
PLANTING DEPTH ½ in (1 cm).
PLANTING DISTANCE Thin to 8–10 in (20–25 cm) apart or plant out when the seedlings have reached 2 in (5 cm) in height. The red-skinned forms are hardier and can be sown in late summer for a winter crop.
SOIL Light, fertile.
SITE Open, sunny.
HARVEST Kohlrabi are ready for eating 8–10 weeks after sowing.
USES Cooked as a vegetable or grated in salads.
OTHER VARIETIES 'Eder', 'Kolibri' (purple), 'Winner'.

Brassica oleracea
Italica Group
Broccoli

The Italica Group of brassicas includes both sprouting and standard broccoli. They grow quite large and ideally a space of 18 in (45 cm) each way should be left between the plants. Some plants will grow 3 ft (90 cm) high. Try growing a few plants of early sprouting broccoli; in warm climates, it produces shoots tasting of asparagus in late winter when they are particularly welcome.

SOW Seed very thinly in mid to late spring.
PLANTING DEPTH ½ in (1 cm). Thin the seedlings and then plant out when they are 3 in (7.5 cm) high.
PLANTING DISTANCE 18 in (45 cm) for white and purple sprouting broccoli; standards can be planted closer, 12 in (30 cm) apart.
SOIL Firm, rich, well drained.
SITE Open, sunny.
HARVEST Pick standard varieties from early summer onwards. Harvest white and purple sprouting broccoli from late summer to early depending on the variety.
USES Delicious kitchen vegetable. Broccoli should be steamed for maximum flavor.
OTHER VARIETIES 'Packman', 'Green Jewel', 'Arcadia', 'De Cicco' (sprouting), 'Minaret' (Romanesco).

Brassica oleracea
Alboglabra Group
Chinese Broccoli

One of a group of vegetables known as Oriental brassicas that are gradually gaining popularity in the West. Oriental brassicas mature more quickly than the traditional cabbages and cauliflowers. Chinese broccoli, also known as gai lohn, is best grown to mature in the fall. It is rather like a cross between standard and purple-sprouting broccoli and the spears are sweet and have a good flavor. They are best steamed or chopped and cooked in a stir-fry.

SOW From spring onwards, but for a fall crop sow in midsummer.
PLANTING DEPTH Sow thinly ½ in (1 cm) deep.
PLANTING DISTANCE Plant out when they are about 3 in (7.5 cm) tall, 10–12 in (20–30 cm) apart.
SOIL Well drained, fertile, moisture retentive.
SITE Open, sunny.
HARVEST Spears will be ready after about 3 months. If sown for a fall harvest they can be picked throughout the early winter.
USES Kitchen vegetable.
OTHER VARIETIES
'Green Lance'.

Brassica rapa
Pekinensis Group
Chinese cabbage

Increasingly available in supermarkets, Chinese cabbages are easy to grow. Because they prefer cool temperatures and shorter days, they are ideal for planting from late summer, when the peas, beans and early potatoes have been harvested. If sown in spring they are likely to bolt. There are two types: the barrel type with a dense heart and the cylindrical 'Michihili' varieties. They can be used in salads, stir-fried, or baked. Boiling destroys their delicate flavor.

SOW Summer. Chinese cabbages resent disturbance and are liable to bolt, so sow them in peat pots, and transplant when the plants have 5 or 6 leaves.
PLANTING DEPTH Sow 3–4 seeds per 3 in (7.5 cm) pot, cover with ½ in (1 cm) of moist compost and thin to the strongest plant if more than one seed germinates.
PLANTING DISTANCE Plant out 10 in (25 cm) apart. Water regularly.
SOIL Good fertile, moisture retentive.
SITE Open, sunny.
HARVEST Chinese cabbages should be ready 8–10 weeks after planting. Cut off at ground level and the stumps will resprout.
USES Salads, kitchen vegetable.
OTHER VARIETIES 'Blues' (napa), 'Minuet' (napa), 'Greenwich' (Michihili).

Brassica rapa
Perviridis Group
Komatsuna

Komatsunas are also referred to as Chinese mustard or spinach mustard. They are closely related to turnips and taste a bit like a cross between cabbage and spinach. They are a prolific and fairly large vegetable so the container gardener needs to allow them a good bit of room. They are quite hardy and will generally survive winter outdoors in warm climates, although they should be given some protection in periods of hard frost. The leaves can be pulled at any time.

Other Chinese brassicas include Pak choi and mitsuna greens; these can be grown in the same way as the species described.

SOW Midsummer in peat pots or in situ.
PLANTING DEPTH ½ in (1 cm).
PLANTING DISTANCE Thin seedlings to 2 in (5 cm) apart if you want to harvest the green when young or space out to 10 in (25 cm) for mature plants.
SOIL Fertile, well drained.
SITE Open, sunny.
HARVEST Leaves should be ready 8 weeks after sowing.
USES As a kitchen vegetable, in salads.
OTHER VARIETIES 'Summer Fest', 'Komatsuna'.

RIGHT *The spreading leaves of a Chinese cabbage; these are becoming increasingly popular as an unusual vegetable.*

Brassica rapa
Rapifera Group
Turnip

Turnips mature quickly and can easily be grown in a small container. They are mainly known as an ingredient of winter stews, but young turnips harvested when the size of golf balls are delicious. Turnip tops, which taste like spinach, can also be eaten. Sow turnips in the early spring for summer harvest and midsummer for fall.

SOW Spring or, for green tops in late winter, late summer/fall.
PLANTING DEPTH ½ in (1 cm).
PLANTING DISTANCE Sow thinly; thin to 5 in (12.5 cm) for early varieties, 9 in (23 cm) for maincrop varieties. Turnips sown for their tops do not need thinning.
SOIL Fertile, well manured. Apply fertilizer before sowing. Do not grow in acid (ericaceous) soil mix. Do not let the soil mix dry out.
SITE Cool, partial shade is best.
HARVEST Early varieties, the best for pots, will be ready in about 6 weeks.
USES Kitchen vegetable. Young plants can be used raw in salads.
OTHER VARIETIES 'Purple Top White Goble', 'Hakurei', 'Tokyo Cross', 'White Lady Hybrid'.

Capsicum annuum
Grossum Group
Sweet Peppers

Sweet peppers are tropical fruit, but new varieties now exist that will flourish in more temperate climates and they are good plants to grow outside on a warm patio. They are popular for use in salads, served with anchovies and capers as a classic Italian starter or stuffed and roasted. They are similar in habit to tomatoes and are grown in the same way, either inside in a greenhouse or outside.

SOW In mid-spring under cover at 70°F (21°C). The seeds will germinate in 14–21 days.
PLANTING DISTANCE If the plants are sown in seed trays, they should be pricked out into pots or cells when three leaves are showing. As they grow they will not require so much heat. Transplant in position when the first flowers show. Water while growing, but take care that the plants do not become waterlogged. Feed when the fruits start to swell.
SOIL Well drained, fertile.
SITE Sheltered, sunny.
HARVEST Picking the fruits when they are green and glossy encourages the plants to produce more fruit; leaving them on the vine to become red lessens the yield.
USES Many as a kitchen vegetable.
OTHER VARIETIES 'Ace' (early), 'Gypsy', 'Yankee Bell'.

LEFT *Sweet peppers can be grown out of doors in a warm sunny position, but the seeds have to be raised under glass in spring.*

Capsicum annuum
Longum Group
Hot peppers

Modern varieties of hot peppers can now be grown in temperate climates provided they are sown under glass and given a sheltered hot position on the balcony or patio. The conditions they require are much the same as sweet peppers. They are an essential ingredient in curries and oriental dishes. Scrape away the seeds when cutting them up. Cooks must however be careful not to rub their eyes after touching raw peppers.

They can be harvested at any time when they are green or red; the longer they stay on the plant and the redder they are the hotter they become. They do not tolerate any frost and the plant must be lifted before the first frosts of winter.

SOW In mid-spring under cover at 70°F (21°C). The seeds will germinate in 14–21 days.
PLANTING DEPTH Sow in seed trays or modules ¼ in (0.5 cm) deep.
PLANTING DISTANCE If the plants are sown in seed trays, they should be pricked out into pots or cells when three leaves are showing. As they grow they will not require much heat. Plant out in position when the first flowers show. Water while growing but take care that the plants do not become waterlogged. Feed when the fruits start to swell.
SOIL Well drained, fertile.
SITE Sheltered, sunny.
HARVEST At any stage after the fruits have formed. The longer they stay on the plant the hotter the peppers become.
USES As a flavoring in curries and oriental dishes.
OTHER VARIETIES 'Early Jalapeno', 'Habanero', 'Big Chile', 'Ancho', 'Serrano', 'Thai Dragon'.

Cichorium endivia
Endive

There are two types of endive: curly-leaved endive, a low-growing plant that looks a bit like curly-headed lettuce, and the broad-leaved Batavian endive, which has broader leaves and makes a more substantial and upright plant. In the kitchen, endive can be used in salads – young, new leaves are best for this – or braised in butter. Traditionally endives are blanched (grown away from light) to make them taste sweeter. Broad-leaved varieties produce attractive white leaves when blanched, although a number of varieties are self-blanching. Endives can be sown in succession from spring through summer and harvested throughout fall and winter.

SOW In trays and plant out, or *in situ*.
PLANTING DEPTH ½ in (1 cm). The seeds will germinate in 3–7 days.
PLANTING DISTANCE Plants should be spaced 10–12 in (25–30 cm) apart, depending on variety. Blanching takes about ten days; cover the plants with an upturned pot or bucket or put a plate over the center of the plant. Traditionally endives were lifted before the first frosts and replanted in a cold frame.
SOIL Fertile, well drained.
SITE Open, sunny.
HARVEST Plants are ready 15–20 weeks after planting. Cut off the head with a sharp knife.
USES Kitchen vegetable or in salads.
OTHER VARIETIES
CURLED 'Bianca Riccia' (for salad mix), 'Neos'.
BROAD-LEAVED 'Batavian Green', 'Casco d'Oro'.

RIGHT Cucumbers have been developed that can be grown outside on a warm patio. They are good plants to grow in growbags.

Cichorium intybus
Chicory

A number of chicories are hardy and make good crops in the winter months, given some protection. Their pale yellow and red leaves add color to salads and they can also be braised. Three main types are grown: Witloof or Belgian chicory, escarole chicory and red chicory, often called radicchio. Witloof chicory is grown in two stages. The seed is sown in late spring and the plants are left to grow until late fall. The leaves are bitter and not usually eaten. In the fall the heads can either be cut off the plants 1 in (2.5 cm) above the ground or the roots can be lifted, trimmed and replanted for forcing indoors. If the roots are left *in situ* they should be covered with soil to a depth of 6–7 in (15–18 cm) and protected with straw or mulch. The tight heads will force their way through the earth. Indoors four roots can be planted in a pot 8–9 in (20–23 cm) and then covered by another pot excluding all light. If they are kept at about 64°F (18°C) the familiar yellow and white "chicons" will be ready in about three weeks. Red and escarole chicory are usually sown in summer to mature in the fall when the heads are cut and used in salads. Some varieties can be forced in the same way as Witloof chicory but these will need winter protection.

SOW Late spring or summer depending on the type being grown.
PLANTING DEPTH ½ in (1 cm).
PLANTING DISTANCE Thin plants to 8 in (20 cm) apart.
SOIL Light, sandy.
SITE Open sunny.
HARVEST Late fall or force in late fall for a winter crop.
USES Salads, as a braised vegetable.
OTHER VARIETIES
WITLOOF 'Apollo', 'Flash', 'Roelof'.
ESCAROLE 'Coral', 'Sugar Loaf Jupiter'.
RED CHICORY 'Fiero' (tall "trevisio" type), 'Chioggia Red Preco No. 1' (Round, "Chioggia" type)

Cucumis sativa
Cucumber

Outdoor cucumbers used to be practically unheard of in cold northern gardens; when they were grown, they produced small, rather bitter misshapen fruits. Modern varieties, however, have changed all this as plant breeders have developed long, smooth cucumbers that tolerate lower temperatures.

SOW Put the seeds on their edge in pots or directly into the soil mix outside. The latter is better, for cucumbers do not like being transplanted. Seeds germinate at 68°F (20°C).
PLANTING DEPTH 1 in (2.5 cm) deep. Sow in groups of three and remove the two weakest seedlings if they all germinate.
PLANTING DISTANCE 18 in (45 cm) apart. Trailing varieties can be grown up string or supports.
SOIL Fertile, moist. Cucumbers need regular watering and feeding with a high-potash feed.
SITE Open, sunny.
HARVEST Cucumbers will be ready about 12 weeks after planting. Cut the fruit frequently, starting when they are about 20 cm (8 in) long or less. The more fruit you cut, the more the plant will produce.
USES Salads, soup, sandwiches. Gherkins (a small form of outdoor cucumber) may be pickled.
OTHER VARIETIES 'Suyo Long' (Chinese), 'Jazzer', 'Marketmore', 'Hokus' (gherkins).

RIGHT Summer Squash or Zucchini are among the easiest plants to grow in containers. In cool weather they may need hand pollenating.

Cucurbita maxima
Pumpkin

Pumpkins belong to the same family as winter squash and zucchinis, and come in a wide range of shapes, sizes and colors. They are not suitable for a patio garden with limited room, but there is no doubt that a traditional orange pumpkin is a triumph for the gardener at Hallowe'en.

SOW As for cucumbers. Sow seeds *in situ* if possible.
PLANTING DEPTH Sow three seeds together, 1 in (2.5 cm) deep with the seeds on their sides. Discard the two weakest plants if all the seeds germinate.
PLANTING DISTANCE Allow 2 ft (60 cm) between plants. Grow trailing varieties either pegged down to the ground or up a tripod. Water in dry weather. Remove all but two or three fruits to achieve maximum size and cut away the leaves to help the fruit to ripen as the pumpkins mature.
SOIL Well drained, moist, fertile.
SITE Open, sheltered.
HARVEST When the skin starts to harden and the stem cracks the fruit is ripe. Cut off the pumpkin with as long a stalk as you can manage and if possible leave in the sun for about a week to cure.
USES The flesh can be used to make pumpkin pie, the pie traditionally eaten at Thanksgiving. The hollowed-out shell is used to make Hallowe'en lanterns with candles alight inside.
OTHER VARIETIES 'Baby Bear' (mini) , 'Wee-B-Little' (bush).
SQUASHES , 'Tuffy' (bush acorn), 'Sweet Dumpling' (small plant).

Cucurbita pepo
Summer Squash

Another member of the cucumber family, summer squash are a widely grown favorite summer vegetable. Those grown in the garden are far better to eat than any bought in a shop. The best summer squash to grow are the compact bush varieties; provided the fruits are harvested regularly, they will continue to produce fruit over a long period.

SOW In the same way as cucumbers. Generally summer squash are raised in pots first, then planted out when the soil is warm and all danger of frost is past. Plants grown in pots should be hardened off by putting them outside during the day before they are finally planted in position.
PLANTING DEPTH 1 in (2.5 cm) deep. Sow in groups of three and remove the two weakest seedlings if all three germinate.
PLANTING DISTANCE 18 in (45 cm) apart. The soil for squash must be well drained and fertile so heap up some garden compost and plant them on top. They need frequent watering.
SOIL Fertile, moist, well drained.
SITE Open, sunny.
HARVEST Squash will be ready 10–14 weeks after planting. Cut the fruit frequently, starting when they are about 4 in (10 cm) long or less. The more fruit you cut, the more the plant will produce.
USES A most popular kitchen vegetable. Squash can be steamed, boiled, fried, baked or eaten raw. The flowers can also be dipped in batter and fried or used in soups.
OTHER VARIETIES 'Raven', 'Yellow Crookneck', 'Revenue'.

Daucus carota
Carrot

If you want to grow carrots in containers, concentrate on those varieties that are short and stumpy rather than the larger winter carrots, which take longer to mature. Give carrots as much depth as possible; they will not grow very well in a shallow growbag. The attractive green foliage makes a pleasing contrast to other vegetables when they are grouped in a trough or planter. More so than with any other vegetable, except possibly peas, a fresh carrot tastes better than anything you can buy.

SOW Seed should be sown very thinly *in situ*. If you like, you can sow seed in cells and then plant them out in position.
PLANTING DEPTH ½ in (1 cm). Carrots need fine, fertile, well drained soil to do well. They also need the soil temperature to be above 45°F (7.5°C) to germinate properly. They have a low nitrogen requirement, so do not grow carrots in soil that has been manured during the past year.
PLANTING DISTANCE Thin maincrop carrots to 1½–2 in (4–5 cm apart). Early carrots grown two seeds to a cell will not require thinning.
SOIL Deep, fine soil, or general-purpose potting compost. Do not let the roots dry out.
SITE Open, sunny.
HARVEST Early carrots are ready 12 weeks after sowing.
USES Favorite kitchen vegetable, especially if eaten when young and tender. Late carrots are stored and used as a vegetable and in soups and stews.
OTHER VARIETIES 'Parmex' (round, small), 'Thumbelina' (round), 'Mokum', 'Little Finger' (all early varieties).

Foeniculum vulgare
Azoricum Group
Florence Fennel

This attractive vegetable, sometimes called sweet fennel, has feathery foliage but it is grown for the aniseed-flavored bulb that develops at the base of the leaf stalks. It is not a particularly easy vegetable to grow and has a tendency to run to seed if its growth is checked in any way. The container gardener will do best to start the plants off in small pots and plant them out in the chosen position when they have four leaves. However, Florence fennel does not like root disturbance and the plants may bolt prematurely. The plant grows to about 2 ft (60 cm) tall and 18 in (45 cm) wide.

SOW Sow seed in early summer; bolt-resistant varieties are best.
PLANTING DEPTH ¹/₂ in (1 cm).
PLANTING DISTANCE 1 ft (30 cm). When the bulbs start to form, earth them up to half their height.
SOIL Fertile, well drained, light sandy soil that does not dry out. They need regular watering when they are growing.
SITE Open, sunny.
HARVEST Plants should be ready after about 15 weeks. Cut off the bulb with a sharp knife, leaving the roots in the soil. Small shoots usually spring from the stump and these can be used in salads.
USES Raw and thinly sliced in salads, braised or boiled.
OTHER VARIETIES 'Cantino', 'Zefa Fino' (bolt resistant), 'Sirio' (sow in July for fall harvesting).

Helianthus tuberosus
Jerusalem Artichoke

The Jerusalem artichoke is a good vegetable for a container garden provided you can devote one good-sized deep container to it. Do not try to grow Jerusalem artichokes in concert with other vegetables or in a grow-bag. They are vigorous plants with attractive green foliage that can reach as high as 10 ft (3 m) in open ground, but are unlikely to reach more than 5–6 ft (1.5–1.8 m) in a container. They may require staking if they are grown in a windy position, and will need watering during the summer. Jerusalem artichokes have a distinctive sweetish taste and a texture similar to that of potatoes. They make delicious soup and can be peeled, boiled and served whole or mashed in the same way as potatoes.

SOW Plant tubers from late winter onwards.
PLANTING DEPTH 4–6 in (10–15 cm).
PLANTING DISTANCE 12 in (30 cm).
SOIL Any. In open ground they are often used to break up heavy soils.
SITE Sun or shade.
HARVEST Cut the foliage down when it starts to go yellow in the fall. The tubers are ready to lift in late fall/early winter when the foliage has died back and are usually lifted as required. The time between planting and lifting is approximately 30–40 weeks.
USES Kitchen vegetable, cook as for potatoes.
OTHER VARIETIES 'Stampede' is high-yielding and extra early with large tubers.

Lactuca sativa
Lettuce

Lettuces are a good standby for the container gardener. They mature quickly, need little room and can be grown in between other vegetables or planted to take the place of crops already harvested. The container gardener is unlikely to fall into the common trap of growing too many at once. Sowings should be planned carefully to ensure as long a supply as possible. Regular watering is necessary throughout the growing period. There are four types of lettuce: butterhead, crisphead, looseleaf and romaine.

SOW Two seeds in a small pot, using as many small pots as necessary. If both germinate, discard the weakest seedling. Harden the plants off by putting them outside before planting in position.
PLANTING DEPTH ¹/₂ in (1 cm).
PLANTING DISTANCE Allow a minimum of 6 in (15 cm) square per plant. The large cabbage crisphead varieties should be allowed more room if it is available.
SOIL Lettuces need fertile, well drained, acid-free soil.
SITE Open, sunny.
HARVEST Looseleaf lettuces are ready for cutting within 6–8 weeks of sowing; cabbage and romaine varieties can take up to four weeks longer depending on the weather and time of year.
USES The salad vegetable supreme, lettuces can also be used to make a delicate summer soup.
OTHER VARIETIES
LOOSELEAF 'Two Star', 'Lollo Rossa'.
BUTTERHEAD 'Nancy', 'Ermosa'.
CRISPHEAD 'Loma', 'Iceberg', 'Anuenue'.
ROMAINE 'Little Gem', 'Winter Density', 'Medallion'.

LEFT *Florence fennel is grown for its succulent bulb. It can be eaten raw or braised or boiled.*

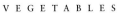

LEFT *Scarlet runner beans are among the best summer vegetables and are easy to grow up tripods of canes in a container.*

Lepidium sativum Cress and *Barbarea verna* Land Cress

Cress is a traditional sprouting crop which many people grow in containers on a windowsill, often on paper. Cultivation and harvesting is virtually the same as for mustard (see page 132). Cress is best grown either in spring or fall, as it goes to seed quickly and does not relish hot weather; the plants should be kept well watered, especially in dry weather. Land, or American, cress is a good alternative to watercress and has a similar flavor. It may also be cooked. It makes a good filler for the container garden; a few seeds can be sown *in situ* either to grow in between other vegetables or as a border around the edge of the container.

SOW A few seeds *in situ* throughout the summer. Seed sown in July and August will provide plants in the fall.
PLANTING DEPTH ½ in (1 cm).
PLANTING DISTANCE Thin plants to 6 in (15 cm) apart.
SOIL Fertile, moisture retentive, rich.
SITE Shade or partial shade.
HARVEST Plants are ready about 8 weeks after sowing. Pick leaves as required.
USES Salads, soups, or cooked as a vegetable.
OTHER VARIETIES Specific varieties not available.

Phaseolus coccineus Scarlet Runner Beans

It might be considered a trifle ambitious to grow scarlet runner beans in a container for they will grow to 10 ft (3 m) but they are relatively simple to grow and the plants can be trained up canes against a wall to form a colorful backdrop with their bright red or red and white flowers and long succulent pods. Dwarf forms are available that grow about 18 in (45 cm) high and are suitable for troughs and windowboxes. For best results these beans need to be grown on very fertile soil and they must be picked continually when the pods start to form. If you let the pods ripen the plant ceases to produce flowers. The container needs to be deep and the soil mix well-fertilized to achieve the best results.

SOW For container-grown plants plant two seeds in a 3 in (7.5 cm) pot of seedling soil mix and discard one if both germinate.
PLANTING DEPTH 2 in (5 cm).
PLANTING DISTANCE Plant out when all danger of frost has passed 9 in (23 cm) apart, water at least once a week when the flowers start to form.
SOIL Rich, fertile, moisture retentive.
SITE Open, sunny, where the shade cast by the plants will not interfere with other vegetables.
HARVEST Beans will be ready to pick approximately 12–14 weeks after planting. Fresh beans will continue to be produced until the first frosts of fall.
USES Favorite kitchen vegetable. Surplus beans can be frozen or salted.
OTHER VARIETIES 'Painted Lady' (red and white flowers), 'Scarlet Emperor'(red flowers), 'Desirée' (white-flowered, stringless), 'Pickwick' (dwarf, stringless).

Phaseolus vulgaris Green Beans

A favorite vegetable in Europe especially France where some varieties are specially grown for shelling and drying as haricots, most beans however are grown for their pods which are cooked and eaten whole. They are best picked and eaten when young. Green beans also freeze well. There are three types of green beans, pencil-podded, usually stringless, flat-podded and wax-pods. Most green beans form bushy plants and these are the ones most suitable for growing in containers. Earth up the stems and water freely when the plants are in flower for best results. The black, yellow and purple varieties now available add interest to a patio garden.

SOW Late spring to midsummer. The seeds will not germinate until the soil temperature reaches 53°F (12°C).
PLANTING DEPTH 1½–2 in (4–5 cm).
PLANTING DISTANCE Sow two seeds every 3½ in (9 cm). Remove one if both germinate and remove every other plant when the plants are established.
SOIL Any.
SITE Sunny, preferably sheltered from strong winds.
HARVEST Late summer, early fall. Time between sowing and picking approximately 8–12 weeks.
USES Excellent summer vegetable.
OTHER VARIETIES 'Provider', 'Jade' (pencil-pod), 'Romanette' (flat-pod), 'Goldkist' (yellow waxpod), 'Purple Queen' (purple waxpod).

Lycopersicon esculentum
Tomato

Outdoor tomatoes are quite easy to grow and are among the best vegetables for the container gardener. They are attractive plants in flower and fruit, but they grow best in relatively warm, sunny climates. In cold, cloudy areas, they can be difficult to grow outside unless they can be offered the protection of a south-facing wall and a sheltered position. Tomatoes can be divided into two types, bush and staking.

The staking varieties are the most common and if they are to grow successfully they need to be trained up a stake or tied to wires. Tie the plants at regular intervals using garden string or raffia and pinch out all the suckers where the leaf stalks join the stem. This leaves you with one straight stem and a number of trusses of fruit. In short season areas, when the fourth truss has developed small tomatoes, pinch out the growing tip two leaves above the truss. This allows the tomatoes to develop and ripen properly. If by any chance the summer ends earlier than it should and you are left with a large number of green tomatoes these can be picked and brought inside and will ripen in the warmth of the house. Alternatively you can use them to make green tomato chutney, a relish prized above many others.

Bush tomatoes are a bit simpler. These varieties grow either as small bushes, as the name implies, or trailing along the ground. They do not require either training or pinching but you do have to cover the ground to prevent dirt or damage to the fruit, a plastic sheet is the easiest thing to use on a patio, as many of the fruits are at ground level. Dwarf tomatoes, plants that grow little more than 8 in (20 cm) high are very suitable for growing in window boxes and small pots but the yield is not large.

The flavor of tomatoes depends on the amount of sunshine they get and the amount of watering and feeding they have received, both of which can reduce the

LEFT *Tomatoes are easy to grow out of doors in a warm spot. They are excellent plants for growbags and should be tied up stakes as the fruits develop.*

flavor. However, all tomatoes grown in containers or growbags need plenty of watering and feeding otherwise the yield will be minuscule.

SOW The container gardener should sow two seeds in a small pot and discard the weaker if both germinate. Many gardeners purchase plants from the local garden center or nursery. This is fine but ensure that the variety is suitable for outdoor cultivation and also one that has a good flavor. A number of the tomatoes traditionally grown for outdoor cultivation fail this test.
PLANTING DEPTH Cover the seeds lightly with seedling soil mix and keep it moist not wet at about 65°F (18°C). Seeds germinate in 8–11 days.
PLANTING DISTANCE Plant out when the first truss of flowers appears and all risk of frost has passed. Harden the plants off before planting out.
SOIL Well drained, reasonably fertile, moisture retentive. Tomatoes are best grown in growbags when they will need watering regularly.
SITE Sunny, sheltered.
HARVEST Tomatoes are ripe when the

fruit turns red. Tomatoes will not stand frost and must be picked before the first frosts of winter. Green tomatoes can be ripened in a cardboard box and some people advocate placing ripe apples alongside them to assist the process.
USES Salad vegetable. The large tomatoes can be de-seeded and stuffed and tomatoes are used in numerous dishes, such as stews, sauces and soups.
OTHER VARIETIES The all-important thing with tomatoes is the variety grown- because it largely determines the flavor of the fruit.
STAKING VARIETIES 'Ruby Cluster', 'Early Cascade', 'Lemon Boy Hybrid' (medium-sized, good flavor); 'Gardener's Delight', 'Sweet 100' (cherry, good flavor); 'Better Boy', 'Celebrity' 'Arkansas Traveler'.
BUSH AND TRAILING VARIETIES 'Container Choice', 'Bonsai Hybrid' (trailing stems, can be grown in a hanging basket), 'Yellow Canary' (dwarf), 'Tiny Tim' (dwarf), 'Teardrop Hybrid' (all have small cherry-like fruit).

Phosocarpus tetragonobolus
Asparagus Pea

An attractive vegetable with scarlet-brown flowers and delicate bluish-green foliage that spreads to form a plant 12–18 in (30–45 cm) high and 18–24 in (45–60 cm) across. Asparagus peas make good plants for the container gardener because they can be planted out individually to fit the container where they are to grow. They grow best in a sunny position in a well-drained soil.

The triangular pods are best harvested when young and should be picked regularly for once the seeds start to harden the growth of the crop is checked. In the kitchen the pods should be cooked whole. They have a flavor of asparagus, hence the name.

SOW Indoors in spring and plant out late spring/early summer. Alternatively, sow seeds outside from mid-spring onwards when the soil has reached 50°F (10°C).
PLANTING DEPTH 1 in (2.5 cm).
PLANTING DISTANCE 10–12 in (25–30 cm) apart.
SOIL Light, rich – so they require feeding when grown in containers.
SITE Open, sunny.
HARVEST From midsummer onwards. Pick the pods when young and immature otherwise they become tough.
USES Culinary.
OTHER VARIETIES Sometimes known as Winged Peas and classified as *Lotus tetragonobolus*.

Pisum sativum
Pea

Peas are one of the commonest and most loved garden vegetables, but they can be maddeningly difficult to grow because they are as popular with birds and mice as they are with humans. They can be difficult to germinate; they do not relish cold soils; and there is no point in sowing them early, particularly in a cold spring, for the mice will have more time to find them and the seeds are prey to fungus and bacterial diseases. Conversely they are a cool weather crop and dislike open and hot positions in the garden. They will grow best in some dappled shade. If you want to grow early peas to mature at the end of May or beginning of June, you should protect the seeds with row cover or mulch.

Peas can be divided into five groups: purple-podded peas (quite rare, but they look attractive in the garden and are well worth considering by the container gardener); snow peas and sugar snaps that are harvested young and the whole pod is cooked and eaten; the small, sweet petit pois; and ordinary garden peas that are shelled (there are two sorts: the sweeter, wrinkle-seeded varieties and the hardier, round-seeded varieties). Finally, there are the semi-leaflesss peas that were originally developed for commercial growers.

Peas will need support as soon as the first tendrils appear. This was traditionally achieved using pea sticks, cut from the hedges or trees. Wide-mesh wire or nylon netting will serve just as well. Peas must be planted in fertile soil to flourish, but thereafter they do not need feeding. They do require watering when they start to flower.

Peas can be grown successfully in containers and should be grown as a feature plant in pots up a decorative trellis. If you plan to do this, check the height of the variety you choose before planting: this can vary from ¹/₂–5 ft (45 cm–1.5 m). If your patio or roof garden is exposed they may require shelter, both from the wind and the birds.

Once the peas start to ripen they should be picked continuously as this encourages the plants to produce more and any surplus can be frozen. Ripe peas should be cooked immediately after picking as the sugar starts to turn into starch once the pod has been picked.

SOW Seeds in spring through to early summer.
PLANTING DEPTH 2 in (5 cm).
PLANTING DISTANCE 3 in (7.5 cm).
SOIL Peas like very fertile soil and will require regular feeding and watering.
SITE Cool. They will not do well on a hot, exposed south-facing terrace.
HARVEST Ready to harvest after approximately 8 weeks.
USES Culinary.
OTHER VARIETIES 'Dakota', 'Knight' (First Earlies), 'Eclipse' (Second Early, holds well), 'Oregon Giant' (snow pea), 'Snowgreen', 'Sugar Snap', 'Sugar Sprint' (stringless snap pea).

RIGHT *A good crop of peas with their attractive white flowers and pale green pods. They should be eaten when young and tender.*

LEFT *Radishes are exceptionally easy to grow and mature extremely quickly. They need to be picked when young because they bolt easily, particularly in hot weather. Sow in succession.*

Raphanus Sativus
Radish

One of the easiest of all vegetables to grow, radishes are the best way to introduce children to gardening. They germinate easily and mature quickly, in about a month. Gardeners with large vegetable gardens often use them as a marker crop to indicate rows of vegetables that take longer to germinate. For the adventurous there are a number of winter-maturing radishes and the giant Japanese mooli radishes. Some varieties can even be grown for their pods but none of these is really suitable for most container gardens. For the container gardener the ordinary globe-shaped summer radish is a good companion plant to grow in pots with lettuces or chard or it can be used as a filler should you want to grow brassicas.

SOW From spring to early summer.
PLANTING DEPTH ½ in (1 cm).
PLANTING DISTANCE Sow seed very thinly where the plants are to grow, about 1 in (2.5 cm) apart is ideal.
SITE Sun or light shade. Do not let the plants dry out or become too crowded.
HARVEST Summer radishes will be ready to harvest after about 4 weeks.
USES As a salad vegetable.
OTHER VARIETIES 'Cherry Belle', 'Scarlet Globe', 'Easter Egg' (mix of red, white and purple).

Sinapsis alba
Mustard

The first half of the traditional school biology project, mustard of 'mustard and cress' fame, is almost the most easily grown vegetable and a welcome addition to salads and sandwiches. Mustard, cress and salad rape (*Brassica napus* var. *napus*) can all be grown with or without soil in dishes indoors and are often found in trays on windowsills. The seeds take about 10–15 days to mature and should then be harvested, cutting the plants off at the base of the stems.

SOW Wash the seeds and then soak them overnight in warm water. Drain and then sprinkle them evenly over several layers of damp kitchen paper. They grow best when sown in spring and fall as the plants run to seed very quickly in hot weather. Keep the paper damp but not waterlogged.
PLANTING DEPTH AND DISTANCE Scatter seeds thinly and evenly over the surface.
SOIL Any, mustard can be grown in soil mix, broadcast or planted in drills as a catch crop in the vegetable garden.
HARVEST 10–15 days after sowing.
USES In salads, of the three vegetables cress is the hottest, mustard is milder and rape is the mildest.
OTHER VARIETIES Other sprouting crops include alfalfa, bean sprouts and fenugreek.

Solanum melongena
Eggplant

The eggplant is a vegetable that needs warmth and protection to grow well but there is no reason why it should not flourish outside provided that you can give it a warm sheltered position in full sun. It is a useful vegetable to start off indoors and then move outside as summer advances. Ideally they should have a minimum day/night temperature of 60–64°F (16–18°C) for growth to continue unchecked. Eggplants have deep roots and should be grown in large containers in a good fertile compost. They should be allowed to develop without forcing and require regular watering during the growing period.

SOW Seed indoors in spring. Seeds require a temperature of 70–86°F (21–30°C) to germinate.
PLANTING DEPTH Plant two seeds in a 3 in (7.5 cm) pot and discard the weakest if both germinate.
PLANTING DISTANCE Plant out in early summer, allowing 18 in (45 cm) between plants. Protect the young plants if the weather is cold. Pinch out the growing tip when the plants are 12 in (30 cm) high. Stake the main stem. In cool climates, pinch off the laterals and flowers when five fruit have set. Eggplant like a humid environment; mist the plants regularly.
SOIL Good, fertile, well drained. Add a potassium-based fertilizer to each feeding once the fruit begin to swell.
SITE Sheltered, sunny.
HARVEST Pick fruit when they have reached 5–6 in (12–15 cm) and the skin is shiny and purple.
USES Eggplants are the main ingredient in the famous Greek dish, moussaka, and also Imam Baaldi, the Turkish vegetable dish that translates as "The priest has fainted". Apparently an epicure was so overwhelmed with the fragrance of the dish when he first came across it that he lost his senses.
OTHER VARIETIES 'Tango' (white skinned), 'Nadia', 'Black Bell'.

Solanum tuberosum
Potato

There will only ever be room for a few potato plants in a patio garden but many people will want to grow one or two in special containers because potatoes grown and eaten straight from the soil are so much better than anything that can be bought in the normal grocery store.

The best potatoes to concentrate on are either the earlies, such as Red Norland, one of the salad potatoes that are so good in the summer, or a plant or two of unusual fingerling potatoes such as Rose Fin Apple with their rosy skins and delicious yellow flesh.

Potatoes can be divided into earlies, second earlies and maincrop and these divisions depend on the number of days that the potatoes take to mature.

Potatoes need to be chitted, or sprouted, before they are planted. Buy seed potatoes in late winter and put them with the rose end (the end with the largest number of eyes) uppermost in an egg carton or a seed tray. Keep them in a light cool room out of the sun. After a few weeks the first shoots will have developed on the tubers. There are two if not three schools of thought about planting potatoes, how deep and how much earthing up is required, but the patio gardener growing them in a container can happily ignore all the controversy.

SOW Maincrop potatoes in the northern hemisphere were traditionally planted on Good Friday. Earlies should be planted two or three weeks earlier but potatoes are not frost-hardy and any young shoots will need protection if frost threatens in late spring.

PLANTING DEPTH Choose a container as large as possible, 12 in (30 cm) wide and deep is a minimum. Special potato planters or old tires, if you can bear to look at them, are ideal. Put some stones in the bottom of the container to provide drainage and then add 4–5 in (10–13 cm)
of soil or compost. Put the chitted potatoes eyes uppermost in the soil mix and then cover them with another 4–5 in (10–13 cm) of soil. When the plants are 6 in (15 cm) high add another 4–5 in (10–13 cm) of soil and repeat this if necessary until the soil is within 2 in (5 cm) of the rim of the pot. Professional gardeners growing potatoes in tires can go on adding tire after tire and filling them with soil mix to obtain a huge yield from two seed potatoes.

PLANTING DISTANCE A minimum-sized container (see above) will accommodate two seed potatoes. Larger containers will grow more on a pro rata basis. Potatoes need regular watering during growth.

SOIL Use good quality potting soil or good garden soil that incorporates a large quantity of compost.

SITE Open, sunny.

HARVEST Lift early potatoes when the flowers open. If growing maincrop potatoes, cut off the stems in early fall and empty the container 10 days later. Do not
leave potatoes in the ground too long as this increases the risk of slug damage. All potatoes should be lifted on a fine day and allowed to dry in the open air for a few hours before they are picked up and stored.

USES Earlies should be boiled and served with mint and butter or cold in salads. Maincrop potatoes can be cooked in so many ways and are used in so many dishes that you need a cook book to explore them.

OTHER VARIETIES Many are available. The following are a selection of recommended varieties.

EARLIES 'Red Sangre' (white flesh), 'Yukon Gold' (yellow flesh), 'Frontier Russet' (white flesh).

MIDSEASON 'Kennebec' (white flesh), 'Carola' (yellow flesh), 'All Blue' (blue flesh).

MAINCROP 'Butte' (Russet skin, white flesh, good for baking), 'German Butterball' (light russet, yellow flesh), 'Island Sunshine' (yellow skin, yellow flesh), 'Desiree' (yellow flesh).

LEFT *When lifting potatoes do it on a dry day and leave the potatoes in the open air for some hours to dry off before lifting and storing them in paper sacks in a cool dry place. If you damage any make sure to use these first.*

Vegetable Recipes

Soups
Borscht

INGREDIENTS
2 onions
2 raw beets
1 oz (30 g) butter
1 can beef consommé
Bouquet garni
Salt, pepper and celery salt
2 cooked beets
*½ cup (125 ml ,4 fl oz) sour cream or
yogurt*
Serves 4–6

1 Chop one onion and both raw beets finely and sweat them in the butter for 15–20 minutes.

2 Add the consommé and bouquet garni and season to taste. Simmer very slowly for about an hour. Strain, leave to cool and skim off any fat.

3 Finely shred half of one of the cooked beets and add it to the soup. Check the seasoning again.

4 Extract the juice from the remaining beet and onion by putting them through a blender or juicer separately and then pressing the juice out through a fine nylon sieve.

5 Reheat the soup to blend the ingredients but do not let it boil or it will change color. Chill the soup and serve cold with a generous spoonful of sour cream stirred into each bowlful just before serving.

Gazpacho

INGREDIENTS
3 cloves garlic
Salt
2 oz (60 g) dried white breadcrumbs
½ cup (125 ml, 4 fl oz) olive oil
3–4 tbsp red wine vinegar
2 small cucumbers
1 red onion
1 red and 1 green pepper
2 lb (900 g) tomatoes
Iced water
Pepper
Chopped chives or marjoram
Croutons for garnish
Serves 4–6

1 Press the garlic through a garlic press and cream with a little salt. Add the breadcrumbs and then work in the olive oil a little at a time. Add vinegar to taste. The final mixture should be quite stiff.

2 Peel the cucumbers and onion and skin the peppers and tomatoes and put them all in a blender. Blend until the mixture is fine and smooth.

3 Mix the breadcrumb mixture with the processed vegetables, season to taste, cover the bowl and chill in the refrigerator.

4 Just before serving, thin the soup with iced water; the exact amount will depend on the juiciness of the tomatoes. Season with pepper and garnish with the herbs and croutons.

Jerusalem artichoke soup

INGREDIENTS
1 lb (450 g) Jerusalem artichokes
1 oz (30 g) butter
1¼ cup (300 ml, ½ pt) each milk and
chicken stock
2 tbsp cream
Salt and pepper
Serves 4–6

1 Scrub and peel the artichokes, cut into slices and fry gently in the butter until soft. Purée in a blender. Mix with the milk and stock and simmer for about 15 minutes.

2 Stir in the cream at the last minute and season to taste.

Sauces
Onion sauce

INGREDIENTS
8 oz (225 g) onions
1½ oz (40 g) butter
½ tbsp plain flour
½ cup (150 ml, ¼ pt) stock or milk
Salt and pepper

1 Slice the onions thinly and cook gently in the butter until soft and translucent.

2 Stir in the flour. Add the stock or milk and simmer slowly until the sauce has thickened. It will take about 10–15 minutes.

3 Process the sauce in a blender until smooth. If the sauce is too thick, add more milk or stock.

Tomato sauce

INGREDIENTS
1 onion, sliced
1½ lb (675 g) ripe tomatoes, skinned
and chopped
½ oz (15 g) butter
1 tbsp olive oil
Salt, sugar and pepper
1 tsp each celery leaves
parsley and basil
1 clove garlic

1 Cook the onion gently in the butter and oil until soft and translucent.

2 Add all the other ingredients and simmer gently for 15–20 minutes, stirring frequently. Process in a blender until smooth. Return the sauce to the pan and reheat.

3 If the sauce is too thin, simmer until it has reduced. Adjust seasoning (do not omit the sugar).

Tomatoes

Main Courses
Simple vegetable curry

INGREDIENTS
1 onion
2 cloves garlic
Cooking oil
1 tbsp ground coriander
1 tsp ground turmeric
1 tsp ground cumin
½ tsp ground chilli powder
½ tsp ground ginger
½ tsp ground mustard seed
Pinch of ground fenugreek (optional)
Vegetables of your choice
Water
Serves 4–6

1 Peel and slice the onion, chop the garlic and fry them in oil until they are soft and translucent.

2 Add all the spices and stir together for 3–4 minutes.

3 Add the prepared vegetables. Cook them gently in the curry mixture and oil for 3–4 minutes.

4 Add water to just cover the vegetables and cook until tender. Add salt to taste.

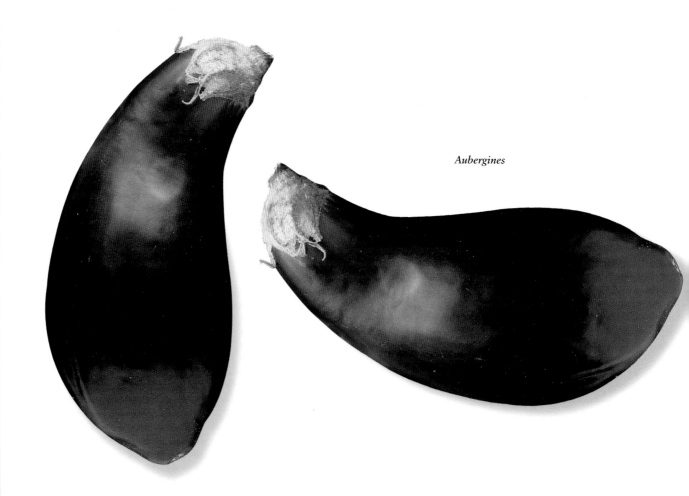

Aubergines

Roast vegetables

INGREDIENTS

1 eggplant

2 zucchini

1 yellow and 2 red peppers

4 tomatoes

3 onions

2 cloves garlic, chopped (optional)

Fresh basil

Olive oil

Salt and pepper

Serves 4–6

1 Preheat the oven to 430°F (220°C, Gas Mark 7). Cut the eggplant and zucchini into chunks, sprinkle with salt and leave the juices to drain for an hour then pat dry.

2 Cut the peppers into large slices and remove the seeds. You can skin them if you wish. Cut the tomatoes in half. Don't skin them. Peel the onions and chop them into chunks.

3 Arrange all the vegetables on a roasting pan, sprinkle with chopped garlic if you wish and basil and season them with salt and pepper. Pour over some olive oil and toss the vegetables in the oil to coat them well on all sides.

4 Roast on the top shelf of the oven for 40 minutes. The vegetables should be just nicely brown at the edges and cooked through.

Ratatouille

INGREDIENTS

2 eggplant

2 zucchini

Salt

4 large tomatoes

2 peppers

2 large onions

Olive oil

2 cloves garlic, chopped

Pepper

Ground coriander

Fresh basil or parsley, chopped

12 black olives, pitted

Serves 4–6

1 Slice the eggplants and zucchini, sprinkle them with salt and leave them to drain for an hour. Skin the tomatoes and deseed and slice the peppers. You can skin the peppers if you wish.

2 Slice the onions. Heat some oil in a large frying pan, and fry the onions gently for 6–7 minutes.

3 Dry the eggplants and zucchini and add them with the peppers and garlic to the onions. You will need to add more olive oil to the pan at this point.

4 Cover and cook gently for 30–40 minutes. Add the chopped tomatoes, season with salt, pepper and ground coriander and cook, covered, for a further 30 minutes until soft. If the ratatouille is too thin, simmer uncovered for the last 10 minutes or so to reduce.

5 To serve hot, mop up any excess oil with a paper towel then sprinkle with basil or parsley. To eat cold, add the black olives and basil or parsley when cool.

Salads
Party salad

INGREDIENTS
Various lettuces: Lollo rossa, arugula, salad bowl, young spinach leaves, red chicory or any combination available.
Streaky bacon
Hard-boiled eggs
Anchovies
Small cherry tomatoes or quartered regular tomatoes
Black olives
Croutons

1 Mix together any combination of young green and red leaves in a large bowl. Fry the streaky bacon until crisp and cut into small pieces. Add the fried bacon together with the bacon fat to the lettuce leaves.

2 Hard boil as many eggs as you require. Peel and cut the eggs into quarters and add to the salad, together with as many tomatoes as you wish. Add a can or two of anchovies, depending on how large your salad is, together with a number of black pitted olives.

3 Stir the bowl thoroughly so that all the ingredients are mixed together and just before serving dress with a good quality salad dressing. Sprinkle croutons generously on top. These ingredients can be varied according to what is available in shops and garden.

Lamb's lettuce

Sweet peppers

1 Take some sweet peppers, preferably red, green and yellow, and remove the skins by putting them on a skewer and holding them over a gas flame until they are charred and black all over. Put them in a plastic bag, allow them to cool, and the skins will rub off fairly easily.

2 Slice the peppers, removing the stalks and the seeds. Lay them in a dish with some anchovies, sliced hard-boiled eggs and capers. Add some olive oil and a few drops of wine vinegar. Season with pepper and decorate with fresh basil. Serve with just a little garlic and olive oil.

Red pepper

Cucumber salad

1 Peel a cucumber and slice it very thinly, preferably with a mandoline. Sprinkle with salt and allow to drain in a colander for 30 minutes with a plate on top to press out the moisture.

2 Lay the slices in a dish in rows, sprinkle with a little white wine vinegar, dress with olive oil and decorate with chopped chives and parsley.

Cucumber

Fruit

Growing fruit in containers is not as difficult or complicated as it might first appear. It is perfectly possible to grow excellent strawberries in one of the specially designed containers that can be purchased at any garden center and, if you wish to grow more permanent trees, new dwarfing rootstocks or semi-dwarfs take up little room. Peaches, plums and apricot trees as well as apples and pears all make good container trees, especially where they can be fan-trained against a south- or west-facing wall. There is enormous satisfaction in growing and eating your own fruit and there is the added bonus that many fruit trees have charming blossoms in the spring. The only fruit not particularly suitable for containers is raspberries.

(NOTE Soil preferences are given for plants grown in open ground. For container gardeners this provides an indication of the type and richness of the most suitable soil mix and growing conditions for that plant.)

Citrus sinensis, C. limon
Orange/Lemon

Many citrus fruits can be grown in containers; in the Edwardian age of sunrooms and glasshouses, oranges and lemons were grown where they could be brought indoors in winter for shelter. Small orange and lemon trees are available and these make excellent plants to decorate a patio in summer. Most citrus trees are frost tender but generally they will survive short periods when the temperature drops to 32°F (0°C). They have attractive sweet-scented flowers and the flowers and fruit are borne on the tree at the same time.

FROST-TENDER Evergreen shrub or small tree (Zones 7–10).
HEIGHT AND SPREAD Mature trees reach 20 ft (6 m) by 10 ft (3m) or more. Container varieties generally have a height and spread of 2 ft (60 cm).
FLOWERS White, fragrant.
FLOWERING Spring to summer.
FOLIAGE Green pointed leaves. Oranges have darker leaves than lemons.
SOIL Moist, well drained, slightly acid.
SITE Full sun.
PROPAGATION Take semi-ripe cuttings in summer.
USES Desserts, drinks, marmalade.
OTHER VARIETIES AND SPECIES
C. aurantium (Seville orange), C. reticulata (clementine), C. sinensis 'Washington' (sweet orange), x Citrofortunella microcarpa (calamondin).

LEFT Lemons are easier to grow in temperate climates than you might think. They can be put outside in the summer and brought indoors in winter.

Cydonia oblonga
Quince

Attractive, rather unusual, fruit trees that can be grown in containers and also make excellent specimen trees in the middle of a lawn. The leaves are a pale, pale light gray-green when they emerge in the spring and the top sides gradually darken as the year progresses. The flowers emerge in late spring and are pale pink to white single flowers, flat and cupped, just like the flowers of the dog rose (Rosa canina) but a bit smaller. They have yellow stamens. The fruit turns from green to gold and should be picked in late fall. Quinces are a tree for a temperate climate for they like cool winters but conversely they flower best in areas with hot summers and in colder areas they should be given the protection of a wall. They can be fan-trained if necessary.

The fruit is not eaten raw, but cooked. When poached, quinces have a bewitching scent that pervades the whole kitchen and they can be used instead of pears, or made into chutney with lemons. The best way to use quinces is to make quince jelly and then use the pulp to make the French sweetmeat cotignac.

HARDY Deciduous small tree or shrub (Zones 5–7).
HEIGHT AND SPREAD 10–15 ft (3–5 m).
FLOWERS Pale pink to white, single.
FLOWERING Late spring.
FOLIAGE Pale gray-green leaves changing to dark green, gray and downy underneath
SOIL Moisture retaining, slightly acid.
SITE Sunny, sheltered.
PROPAGATION Chip-budding or hard-wood cuttings in summer.
USES Jelly, chutney, poached fruit.
OTHER VARIETIES 'Lusitanica', (dark yellow fruit), 'Meech's Prolific' (golden-yellow pear-shaped fruit), 'Vranja' (fragrant pale green fruit).

Ficus carica
Fig

A fig is a good tree to grow in a container, which restricts its growth and increases the fruit yield. Figs are semi-tropical, but the common fig can be grown out of doors in temperate climates in any reasonably warm situation.

In a warm climate they will fruit twice a year – an early crop and a main crop in late summer. In cooler climates they carry only one crop. The embryo fruits formed at the end of the previous summer will benefit from some protection over the winter.

Figs are best grown as fans against a wall, and the fruit is formed on first- and second-year wood. To encourage this wood, cut back every alternate lateral that has fruited on the main branches to one bud in fall. In summer, stop all new growth at 4–5 leaves and tie in all new shoots. Cut away surplus growth to allow the sun to ripen the fruit, and try to leave 6–9 in (15–23 cm) between each shoot.

HARDY Deciduous tree (Zones 5–7).
HEIGHT AND SPREAD 10 ft (3 m) by 12 ft (3.5 m).
FLOWERS None.
FOLIAGE Large, dark green, 3- or 5-lobed leaves.
SOIL Moist, well drained.
SITE Sunny, sheltered.
PROPAGATION Hardwood cuttings taken from one-year-old wood or sever suckers from the parent tree.
USES Late summer fruit.
OTHER VARIETIES 'Improved Brown Turkey', the most commonly grown, 'Adam', 'Alma', 'Brunswick', 'Celestial', 'Sultane', 'White Ischia', 'White Marseilles'.

RIGHT *'Discovery' is one of the most popular early apples, delicious and crisp. It will not keep and should be eaten right away.*

Malus domestica
Apple

Apple trees can be trained into a number of forms to fit into any patio garden design. Very dwarfing rootstocks may seem a good choice for a container, but a more vigorous one is better if you are planning to train the tree as a fan against a wall. Dwarf trees fruit on small spurs carried on a main stem. They reach 6–8 ft (1.8–2.4 m) tall and can be planted 2 ft (60 cm) apart.

Apples are grown for their fruit which ripens from late summer into the fall depending on the variety, but they have the bonus that apple blossom is possibly the loveliest of all garden flowers in late spring.

Apples grown in containers will need watering, all apples need pruning, and all apples trained as cordons or fans need a firm structure of wire to which they can be tied. Apples trees are either tip-fruiting or spur fruiting; buy a spur-fruiting variety if you plan to train the tree as a fan or cordon.

HARDY Small tree (Zones 4–6).
HEIGHT AND SPREAD Various.
FLOWERS Pink and white blossom.
FLOWERING Spring.
FOLIAGE Green, pointed at both ends.
SOIL Fertile, well drained.
SITE Open, sunny.
PROPAGATION Chip budding or grafting.
USES Eating raw or cooking.
OTHER VARIETIES
EATING APPLES 'Discovery' (partial tip-bearer), 'Egremont Russet', 'Tydeman's Early Worcester' (early–mid season), 'Cox's Orange Pippin', 'Jonagold', 'Idared', 'Laxton's Superb' (late season).
COOKING APPLES 'Arthur Turner', 'Bismarck', 'Lord Derby', 'Rev. W. Wilks' (mid season), 'Bramley's Seedling' (partial tip-bearer), 'Monarch' (late season).

Mespilus germanica
Medlar

Another unusual fruit tree that can be used as a decorative tree in a container. Medlars have much the same requirements as quinces and they are often presented with them in fruit catalogs. They have large oblong or oval dark green leaves that turn yellow and brown in the autumn, and a weeping habit. They have attractive large white or pink-tinged flowers and should be treated and pruned as standard apple trees. The fruits of the medlar are rather strange and look a bit like overlarge rose hips. They are left on the tree until they are really ripe and are eaten when "bletted" (partially rotten). They are an acquired taste. Medlars are most often used to make medlar jelly, an astringent preserve that is an excellent accompaniment to roast meat.

HARDY Deciduous small tree or large shrub (Zones 4–6.)
HEIGHT AND SPREAD 12 ft (3.5 m).
FLOWERS Large white single 5-petalled flowers, tinged with pink.
FLOWERING Late spring.
FOLIAGE Dark green, long oblong.
SOIL Fertile, moist, well drained.
SITE Sun, partial shade.
PROPAGATION Budding or whip-and-tongue grafting.
USES Preserves or eaten raw.
OTHER VARIETIES 'Dutch', 'Monstrous', 'Nottingham'.

LEFT *Morello cherries are excellent trees for a shady north wall. They are popular with birds and may need netting.*

Physalis edulis
Cape Gooseberry

A close relative of the decorative Chinese or Japanese lantern *P. alkekengi*, Cape Gooseberries are welcome for both their decorative and edible qualities. The fruit can be eaten raw but is often used to make jam. Suitable for containers, the plants grow as high as 6 ft (1.8 m), with a number of branches. The fruits form in the nodes of the branches following the white flowers.
CAUTION flowers and fruits of *P. alkekengi*, Chinese lantern, should not be eaten as they can cause stomach upsets.

PERENNIAL Usually grown as an annual. (Zones 7–10)
SOW Indoors in late winter/early spring at a temperature of 65–70°F (18–21°C).
PLANTING DEPTH ½ in (1cm).
PLANTING DISTANCE Prick out seedlings into 3 in (7.5 cm) pots and then pot individual plants into 6 in (15 cm) pots in which they will bear fruit.
SITE Sheltered, sunny site or greenhouse.
SOIL Any, well drained.
HARVEST Fall when the calyces (the papery outer casing) have changed from green to golden brown.
USES Culinary.
OTHER VARIETIES None.

Prunus armeniaca
Apricot

One of the most delicious of the summer tree fruits, apricots are exacting in their requirements, but well worth the trouble. They need a relatively long period of cool weather over the winter but blossom very early in the year when, in many areas, they require protection against late frosts; the lovely pink flowers appear on the naked branches before the leaves. They then need warmth and sun to ripen the fruit, so in temperate climates they are best grown as a fan against a west- or south-facing wall. Apricots are also prone to die-back. An apricot that has been grafted onto a seedling peach rootstock is best for a container; these produce smaller trees and withstand wet conditions better.

Bush trees should be pruned as for plums, as they fruit on one-year-old shoots and older fruiting spurs, but a fan-trained apricot should be pruned as for a peach.

FROST-HARDY Deciduous tree (Zones 5–8).
HEIGHT AND SPREAD Mature fan trees can reach 20 ft (6 m) across. Smaller fans may reach 12 ft (3.5 m) after several years.
FLOWERS Pink, shallow, cupped, borne in clusters.
FLOWERING Early–mid-spring.
FOLIAGE Single, pointed, alternate, green.
SOIL Fertile, well drained, slightly alkaline.
SITE Sunny, sheltered.
PROPAGATION Budding.
USES Eaten raw, preserves and sauces. Apricots will not keep but they can be frozen.
OTHER VARIETIES 'Blenheim', 'Early Moor Park', 'Moor Park', 'Earlicot'.

Prunus avium,
P. cerasus
Sweet and acid cherries

Until recently, only acid-cherry varieties were suitable for growing in containers. Few sweet cherries were self-fertile and they had not been grafted reliably on to any small rootstock. The development of the Inmil rootstock means that a fan-trained cherry can be planted that requires a space of only 6 ft (1.8 m) high by 12 ft (3.6 m) wide; a number of self-fertile varieties have also been developed, such as 'Lapins' syn. 'Cherokee' and 'Stella'. The favorite acid cherry, 'Morello' needs about the same space as an Inmil fan-trained tree but has the advantage that it flowers and fruits best when grown against a north-facing wall.

Cherries grown in containers against a wall have one enormous advantage: a net can be placed over the ripening fruit to protect it from the depredations of birds. In many gardens where cherries are grown in the open, few survive.

Sweet cherries flower on spurs of old wood and should be pruned and trained as for plums. Morello cherries fruit on one-year-old wood and should be pruned and trained as for peaches.

HARDY Deciduous tree (Zones 4–6).
HEIGHT AND SPREAD 6 ft (1.8 m) by 12 ft (3.6 m).
FLOWERS Pink or white blossoms.
FLOWERING Mid-spring to early summer. Early-flowering varieties may need protection from late frosts.
FOLIAGE Pointed green leaves that often turn red, gold and yellow in fall.
SOIL Fertile, well drained.
SITE Sunny, sheltered for sweet cherries, north walls for acid cherries.
PROPAGATION Grafting.
USES Fresh fruit, jams and preserves.
OTHER VARIETIES AND SPECIES
SWEET *P. avium* 'Lapins' syn. 'Cherokee', *P. a.* 'Stella', *P. a.* 'Chelan'.
ACID: *P. cerasus* 'Montmorency', *P. c.* 'Morello', *P. c.* 'Nabella'.

Prunus domestica, P. institia
Plums, gages and damsons

Any of the plums or gages are a good choice to grow on a sheltered patio, for they flower early and plum blossoms often need protection against the late-spring frosts. Choose varieties grafted on to Pixy (dwarfing) rootstocks, and make sure that the variety you choose is self-fertile – some are not.

In some years the trees may bear an overload of fruit. This should be thinned or the branches may break under the weight. Also plums should be pruned in summer, particularly in temperate climates, for this makes them less liable to silver-leaf disease.

There are many fine varieties available, so just choose the one you prefer, or whose fruit is difficult to obtain locally. If you have room for only one tree, choose one of the luscious dessert varieties. Grown in a container, they should be trained as a fan against a warm wall.

HARDY Deciduous tree (Zones 4–6).
HEIGHT AND SPREAD 6 ft (1.8 m) by 12 ft (3.6 m).
FLOWERS White blossom.
FLOWERING Mid-spring.
FOLIAGE Medium-sized, pointed, green.
SOIL Fertile, well drained.
SITE Sheltered, sunny.
PROPAGATION Grafting.
USES Eating and cooking. Damsons make particularly delicious jam.
OTHER VARIETIES AND SPECIES
DESSERT PLUMS AND GAGES
P. domestica 'Cambridge Gage',
P. d. 'Yellow Gold', *P. d.* 'Cherry Red',
P. d. 'Burbank'.
COOKING PLUMS *P. d.* 'Czar',
P. d. 'Pershore', *P. institia* 'Bradley's King Damson', *P. i.* 'Prune Damson'.

Prunus persica
Peach

In warm climates, peaches are best grown as bushes; in less favorable areas they are normally grown as fan-trained trees against a warm south- or south-west-facing wall.

To grow a fan-trained peach on a patio four things are essential: at least 6 ft (1.8 m) by 12 ft (3.6 m) of wall; a firm framework of wires on to which you can tie canes; time and patience to establish the fan; and an understanding of the pruning requirements, as peaches fruit on the previous year's wood.

Most peaches are grafted onto St Julian A rootstock, but there are also dwarfing varieties that can be grown as bushes in tubs. Peaches are also exacting in their requirements for spraying against disease (particularly leaf curl), fertilizing, and watering. When successful the fruit needs thinning carefully.

HARDY Deciduous tree (Zones 5–7).
HEIGHT AND SPREAD 6 ft (1.8 m) by 12 ft (3.6 m).
FLOWERS Pink blossom.
FLOWERING Spring.
FOLIAGE Fairly long, green and pointed with a yellow central rib.
SOIL Well drained, fertile.
SITE Sunny, sheltered.
PROPAGATION Grafting or budding.
USES Eaten raw, or used for jam.
OTHER VARIETIES
WHITE 'Duke of York', 'Peregrine'.
YELLOW 'Hale Haven', 'Earliglo', 'Stellar'.
DWARF 'Bonanza', 'Garden Lady'.

Prunus persica var. *nectarina*
Nectarine

The growing requirements of the smooth-skinned nectarine are almost identical to the peach, although nectarines are slightly more tender. Planting, pruning and training are the same for both. Nectarine blossom appears early and may need protection against late frosts. Because there may be few pollinating insects around, it is helpful to self-pollinate the trees, choosing a dry day and transferring the pollen from flower to flower with a fine artist's paintbrush. Constant watering in summer is essential. Nectarines need feeding with liquid fertilizer if there is a heavy crop; feeding should not be started until the fruit has passed the stoning stage and should be discontinued once the fruit has started to color.

HARDY Deciduous tree (Zones 5–7).
HEIGHT AND SPREAD 6 ft (1.8 m) by 12 ft (3.6 m).
FLOWERS Pink blossom.
FLOWERING Spring.
FOLIAGE Fairly long, green and pointed with a yellow central rib.
SOIL Well drained, fertile, loamy.
SITE Sunny, sheltered.
PROPAGATION Grafting or budding.
USES Eaten raw, or used for jam.
OTHER VARIETIES 'April Glo', 'May Kist', 'Earliglo', 'Nectarella' (dwarf variety).

RIGHT Nectarines are slightly more delicate than peaches but can be grown outside given the protection of a south-facing wall.

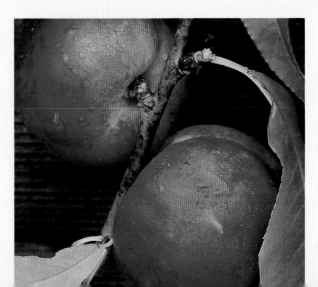

Training fruit trees

Cordons

Cordons are single stemmed trees – fruiting spurs grow directly from the main stem – although double or even triple cordons can be created. Apple and pear cordons are generally planted at an angle of 45° and trained to a height of 6 ft (1.8 m). This produces a stem 8 ft (2.4 m) long. All cordons should be pruned in the summer; little winter pruning is necessary. Pruning is simple. Cut back all laterals (side branches) to three buds beyond the basal cluster (the cluster of leaves nearest the main stem). Tie in the leader but do not prune it until it has reached 6 feet in height. Mature cordons may need some of the fruiting spurs thinned in the course of time.

Espaliers

Espaliers are trees with branches radiating horizontally from a main stem – the fruit grows from spurs on the radiating branches. Before planting the tree, erect a horizontal wire framework with the wires 15–18 in (38–45 cm) apart.

To create an espalier, plant a whip (a young single-stemmed tree) in fall. In spring, cut back the stem to a bud about 2 ft (60 cm) above the ground, making sure that there are two further buds below the top one. The tree will produce three shoots in the summer. Tie in the top one vertically and tie the two side shoots in at an angle of 45°. Summer prune

any other shoots that emerge to three leaves from the basal cluster.

In the spring of the second year, cut back the leader again to three good buds and take down the first two side shoots from 45° to the horizontal. Tie the shoots on to canes attached to the wires. Repeat this each year until the tree has reached the desired height and spread. At this point the extension leaders should be stopped and the lateral shoots treated as if they were cordons.

Fan-trained plum tree

To save time, try to buy what is known as a feathered maiden, – a whip with side shoots – and plant it in the fall. In late spring, cut back the central stem to the uppermost of two strong opposing laterals. Train these horizontally against the wall; the top side shoots should be about 2 ft (60 cm) above the ground. Tie these shoots in, then cut them back by a half to an upward-facing bud. They form the first ribs.

During the summer, select two new upward-growing shoots and one downward-growing shoot from each branch, spaced evenly along the rib. Tie these in and pinch back any other side shoots to 1–2 leaves. Rub out any shoots growing inwards towards the wall or outwards.

The following spring, cut back the new ribs by between a half and a third and during the summer select three new shoots from each of these. Continue this process on an annual basis until the tree has taken up its allotted space.

After the fan is established annual prun-

ing consists of rubbing out any shoots that are growing in the wrong direction, pinching back new laterals to 6–7 leaves in midsummer to help form fruit-bearing spur systems and the shortening of the laterals to 3 leaves when the fruit has been picked. Apricots should be trained and pruned in the same way.

Plums must only be pruned from late spring through summer as otherwise they are prone to silver-leaf disease which usually proves fatal.

Other fan-trained trees

The establishment of a fan-trained peach tree is exactly the same as a plum tree for the first two years but the pruning and training of mature trees differs after that.

In the third year side shoots should be allowed to grow from the ribs every 6 in (15 cm) or so both on the top and underside of the rib. Tie these shoots in, and stop them when they have reached 18 in (45 cm) long. Pinch out all other shoots at 1–2 leaves. After fruiting the shoots that have borne fruit are cut out back to the new replacement shoots that have been tied in.

In the spring on mature trees the young shoots bearing blossoms will have two buds at their base. These form replacement shoots and one of the buds needs to be rubbed out to prevent the tree from becoming congested. Keep another bud growing from the middle of the shoot as a reserve. Once the tree has reached its allotted span pinch back any terminal growth to 4 leaves once it has made 6 leaves.

CORDONS

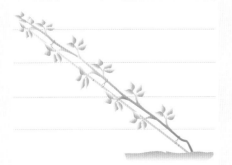

ESPALIERS

FAN-TRAINED TREES

Fragaria × ananassa
Strawberry

Strawberries are excellent fruit for the patio gardener and are especially attractive grown in special strawberry planters or tubs, producing their white flowers in late spring and delicious red fruits that ripen in summer. They can also be raised in growbags, planted in late summer to bear fruit the following year. It is possible to retain strawberry plants in growbags for two years but it is probably best if they are replaced annually. There are a large number of strawberry varieties available.

Strawberries are a greedy crop. They need to be planted in well drained soil that has been well manured the previous year and do best in slightly acid soil. They also require watering in dry periods if they are to fruit properly. The yield from a strawberry plant starts to decline after the third year and plants should be replaced on a regular basis to compensate for this.

RIGHT The best-loved summer fruit that can be grown in containers as long as there is sufficient sun to ripen the fruit properly.

Summer-fruiting strawberries are usually divided into early, mid or late season. If there is room, then an early and a mid-season variety can be grown together; this will prolong the period when fresh fruit can be enjoyed. However, a number of varieties fruit early in their first year and then revert to mid-season.

Some varieties are known as day neutral strawberries. These have a small number of berries in late spring or summer, and then fruit again in the fall, when they may carry produce over a considerable period. These strawberries succeed best in warmer areas where there is less likelihood of early frosts in the fall. Unlike the standard summer plants, the runners of day neutral varieties should be retained and the major weeding and removal of old leaves is carried out at the end of winter, just before the new growth starts.

Wild or Alpine strawberries can be planted in troughs on a patio where they make good ground-cover plants. They can also be planted in between paving slabs and are an attractive addition to a patio. They are hardier than most strawberries and prefer cool shade, they do not do well in a dry, sunny position.

HARDY Creeping perennial (Zones 4–6).
HEIGHT AND SPREAD 6 in (15 cm) by 12 in (30 cm).
FLOWERS White occasionally pink, with pronounced yellow centers, held in clusters.
FLOWERING Late spring.
FOLIAGE Green, slightly hairy, toothed edges with three leaflets per leaf. The leaves often turn brilliant red in the fall.
SOIL Slightly acid, fertile, well drained.
SITE Open, sunny.
PROPAGATION Cut off and replant rooted runners.
USES Popular summer fruit with many uses in the kitchen.
OTHER VARIETIES
EARLY 'Elvira', 'Honeoye', 'Annapolis' 'Northeaster'.
MID AND LATE SEASON 'Sparkle', 'Jewel' (late), 'Seneca', 'Allstar' , 'Mira', 'Mesabi', 'Primetime'.
DAY NEUTRAL 'Tristar', 'Tribute', 'Chandler'.
ALPINE 'Improved Rugen'

GROWING STRAWBERRIES IN TUBS OR BARRELS

This is an excellent way to produce a good crop of strawberries in a small space, but two important rules need to be observed. First, prepare the correct planting mixture, which should be equal parts by volume of sharp sand (or vermiculite) and a good quality garden potting soil. Make sure that the soil mix contains a slow-release fertilizer, or add one if it does not. Second, place a perforated pipe down the center of the barrel or use a specially designed container with a central watering tube. Unless this is done, the plants at the bottom of the containers will not receive sufficient water and will probably die. Plant up the barrel at the same time as it is filled with the planting mixture, pushing the plants through the holes from the inside and ensuring that the crown of each plant is level with the sides of the barrel. Water the barrel well after planting and then do not water again for around two to three weeks – however, the plants must not be allowed to become so dry that they show signs of wilt. Less water is required when the plants are small than later when they are in full growth but too much water and, likewise too much fertilizer, may well just produce leaves rather than fruit. Rotate the tubs or barrels every week so that the plants receive equal sunlight.

Protection against birds and squirrels
The main problem with growing strawberries is protecting the crop against birds and squirrels, who can strip a bed of unripe fruit overnight. Birds can usually be kept off by adequate netting, but if your patio is infested with squirrels only a really stout wire cage will suffice to keep them at bay.

Pyrus communis
Pear

The growing, pruning and training requirements of pears are much as for apples, although the early blossoms are more liable to be damaged by late frosts. If possible, pears should be placed against a south- or south-west-facing wall. Train as a cordon.

For a container, choose pears grafted on to Quince C or Quince A rootstock for they are less vigorous, Quince C being the most dwarfing. Dwarf trees are also available and these are most suitable for planting in containers. It is advisable to plant two pear trees of different varieties, as pears are not reliably self-fertile and two compatible trees are often needed if they are to bear fruit.

HARDY Deciduous tree (Zones 5–7).
HEIGHT AND SPREAD A fan-trained
Quince C rootstock will reach 6 ft (1.8 m)
by 12 ft (3.6 m) in 8–10 years.
FLOWERS White blossoms, borne in
clusters.
FLOWERING Spring.
FOLIAGE Single, green, pointed.
SOIL Well drained, fertile.
SITE Sunny, sheltered.
PROPAGATION Budding or grafting.
USES Eaten raw, or cooked.
OTHER VARIETIES
Letters show compatible flowering groups.
'Concorde' (C), 'Conference' (C), 'Doyenné
du Comice' (D), 'Onward' (D), 'Williams'
Bon Chrétien' (C).

Ribes nigrum
Blackcurrant

Currants grow well in temperate countries and blackcurrants are an excellent choice for they can be used to make jam, jellies and syrups as well as in a large variety of summer desserts. All currant bushes require about 4–5 ft (1.2–1.5 m) of space.

Blackcurrants fruit mainly on the previous year's wood and should be pruned hard in late fall to promote the growth of new wood the following year. On established bushes, remove three old branches entirely and cut back other branches that have borne fruit to a strong lateral side branch. Remove damaged or weak branches. It is easy to tell the age of the wood on a blackcurrant bush: new wood is very pale brown, two-year-old wood is gray and old wood is black. Feed with compost and nitrogen and potassium fertilizers in early spring.

HARDY Deciduous shrub (Zones 4–6).
HEIGHT AND SPREAD 4 ft (1.2 m) by
5 ft (1.5 m).
FLOWERS Pale green, insignificant,
carried in tresses.
FLOWERING Spring.
FOLIAGE Dark green, heart-shaped with
three lobes.
SOIL Fertile, well drained. Blackcurrants
do poorly on badly drained soil.
SITE Sheltered, sun or partial shade.
PROPAGATION Hardwood cuttings from
that year's wood in fall.
USES Preserves, summer desserts, freezes
well.
OTHER VARIETIES 'Ben Sarek' (small),
'Titania', 'Ben Lomand'.

LEFT *Conference pears are the hardiest and most suitable for northern gardens. They keep well if stored in a cool place.*

Ribes rubrum
Redcurrant and whitecurrant

Whitecurrants are a color variant of redcurrants. The two are normally grown on a "leg" with a number of lateral branches radiating from a stem. They are easily trained in cordons, fans or espaliers. Cordons occupy much less room than an open bush.

To train the bush as a vertical cordon, cut back all laterals to within 1 in (2.5 cm) of the main trunk in winter and cut back the main leader to within 6 in (15 cm) of last year's growth. In summer, cut back the laterals of all new growth to 4–5 leaves to help to form spurs. Repeat until the cordon has reached the height that you wish.

Redcurrants grown as bushes should be pruned twice a year. In summer, cut back small and unwanted branches to within 4 in (10 cm) of the main stem to allow light to reach the fruit. In winter, shorten all the leaders by about half to an outward pointing bud.

The growing requirements are the same as for blackcurrants. All currants benefit from an application of potassium-based fertilizer in the spring.

HARDY Deciduous shrub (Zones 4–6).
HEIGHT AND SPREAD 90 cm (3 ft) by
4 ft (1.2 m).
FLOWERS Pale green, insignificant,
carried in tresses.
FLOWERING Spring.
FOLIAGE Mid green, heart-shaped with
three lobes.
SOIL Fertile, well drained. Red and white-
currants will tolerate heavier soils than
blackcurrants.
SITE Sheltered, sun or partial shade.
PROPAGATION Hardwood cuttings in
fall.
USES Desserts, jams and jellies.
OTHER VARIETIES
RED: 'Jonkheer van Tets', 'Laxton Number
One', 'Pink Champagne', 'Red Lake',
'Redstart', 'Rovada'.
WHITE: 'White Versailles', 'White Grape',
'White Transparent', 'Blanca'.

Ribes uva-crispa var. *reclinatum*
Gooseberry

Gooseberries have a lot in common with redcurrants. They are easy to grow but they will not flourish in a hot dry position and some shade is essential. They are a good fruit bush to try on a shaded patio but it may be best to train them against a wall as a cordon or espalier, for their spines are long and sharp and care needs to be taken when handling, them unless you grow the red variety 'Captivator' which is almost thornless. Cordon and fan-trained gooseberries are treated the same way as redcurrants. It is worth noting that gooseberries vary greatly in their yield according to the soil conditions that prevail. It is therefore worth consulting a local specialist or nursery to see which varieties do best where you live.

Gooseberries are the first fruit of the season and are most welcome in the kitchen for their tart refreshing flavor. They are best stewed or as gooseberry fool. Dessert gooseberries should be left on the bush to mature and the fruit should be thinned and the first pickings used for cooking. The modern introduction 'Invicta', which is immune to American gooseberry mildew, is possibly the best cooking gooseberry available.

HARDY Deciduous shrub (Zones 4–6).
HEIGHT AND SPREAD 2½ ft (75 cm) by 3 ft (90 cm).
FLOWERS Insignificant, pale green.
FLOWERING Spring.
FOLIAGE Green, small, currant-like.
SOIL Any, fertile, well drained.
SITE Sun, partial shade.
PROPAGATION Hardwood cuttings in fall.
USES Cooking or dessert.
OTHER VARIETIES 'Careless', 'Invicta', 'Leveller', 'Hinnonmaki Red' (red).

Rubus fruticosus
Blackberries and hybrid berries

Cultivated blackberries and hybrid berries are easy to train, crop prolifically and just require space against a fence or wall supported by a framework of wires. The thornless varieties are generally less vigorous, making them suitable for container growing.

These berries fruit on one-year-old wood and produce new growth from the base each year. This growth should be tied in, usually in the center of the fruiting branches. When fruiting is over, the old canes are cut off at ground level and the new canes attached to the wire framework in a fan, rope or woven shape – weaving is generally the most satisfactory method.

HARDY Deciduous climbers (Zones 4–6).
HEIGHT AND SPREAD 6 ft (1.8 m) by 8 ft (2.4 m); 'Bedford Giant', 'Fantasia', 'Silvanberry' and 'Sunberry' require double this.
FLOWERS Small white blossoms.
FLOWERING Spring.
FOLIAGE Generally green, heart-shaped, with serrated edges and pronounced point, held in groups of three on a stalk.
SOIL Fertile, well drained.
SITE Sheltered, sun or partial shade.
PROPAGATION Tip layering or leaf bud cuttings.
USES Eating raw, jams and jellies, desserts.
OTHER VARIETIES
BLACKBERRIES 'Illini Hardy', 'Chester', 'Triple Crown', 'Oregon Thornless', 'Waldo' (thornless).
HYBRIDS 'Boysenberry', 'Japanese Wineberry', 'King's Acre Berry', Loganberry 'LY 654', Tayberry, 'Veitchberry'.

RIGHT *Highbush blueberries such as 'Blue Crop' are becoming increasingly popular. They must be grown in acid soil.*

Vaccinium corymbosum
Blueberries

Highbush blueberries and their near relatives, cranberries (*V. macrocarpon*) and bilberries (*V. myrtillus*), can easily be grown in tubs on a patio provided the compost used has a pH of between 4.0 and 5.5; they will not tolerate alkaline soil. They all like cool moist conditions. For blueberries, it is a good idea to grow two varieties as this will improve pollination. The species have different growth habits: blueberries form a substantial bush, while the two related species are creeping shrubs, sometimes used as ground-cover plants. Established highbush blueberries should be pruned in winter, removing some old branches to ground level and all side branches growing in a sideways or downwards direction.

HARDY Deciduous shrub (Zones 3–5).
HEIGHT AND SPREAD 5 ft (1.5 m).
FLOWERS White or pink tinged, held in clumps.
FLOWERING Late spring.
FOLIAGE Green, pointed, oval.
SOIL Acid, well drained.
SITE Sun or partial shade, sheltered.
PROPAGATION Softwood cuttings in midsummer.
USES Eaten raw, used in cakes and desserts.
OTHER VARIETIES 'Bluecrop', 'Coville', 'Earliblue', 'Herbert', 'Ivanhoe', 'Patriot'.

Fruit Recipes

Spiced peaches

INGREDIENTS

*1 tsp each ground cinnamon, allspice
and coriander
½ tsp each ground nutmeg and cloves
8 oz (225 g) granulated sugar
1 lb (450 g) fairly firm peaches
½ cup (125 ml ,4 fl oz) white wine
vinegar*
Serves 6–8

1 Mix the ground spices with the sugar. Plunge the peaches into boiling water to loosen the skins, then peel.

2 Cut the peaches in half, remove pits, place in a pan and cover with the sugar and vinegar. Bring slowly to the boil, then simmer until the fruit is cooked – no more than 2–3 minutes.

3 Remove the fruit from the saucepan with a slotted spoon and place in jars with tightly fitting lids.

4 Boil the vinegar mixture until it starts to thicken and then pour it over the fruit. Seal the jars and leave the peaches to mature. Serve as an accompaniment to cold ham, pork or turkey.

Summer pudding

INGREDIENTS

*8 oz (225 g) blackcurrants
12 oz (350 g) caster sugar
8 oz (225 g) redcurrants
4 tbsp water
1 lb (450 g) raspberries
Unsalted butter, for greasing
Loaf of fresh white sliced bread
Whipped cream to serve*
Serves 6–8

1 Poach the blackcurrants in a saucepan with one-third of the sugar and 4 tablespoons water, very, very gently, without stirring and making as little juice as possible; it is only necessary for the sugar to dissolve. Poach the redcurrants separately in the same way. Leave to cool.

2 Place the raspberries in a bowl and sprinkle them with the remaining sugar; set aside for 30 minutes.

3 Grease the sides of a 2 pint (1 litre) pudding basin with butter. Cut the crusts off the bread and arrange the slices so that they cover the sides and bottom of the pudding basin completely.

4 Mix the red and blackcurrants together and then add the fruit in layers to the basin, alternating currants and raspberries. Put a layer of bread between each layer of fruit. Do not add very much juice. Reserve any remaining juice in a jug.

5 When the basin is full, cover with a layer of bread, making sure there are no gaps. Put a plate on top with a weight to press the pudding down and refrigerate overnight.

6 To serve, turn out on to a plate and use the reserved juice to color any white bread. Serve with whipped cream.

Blueberry pie

INGREDIENTS

FOR THE SHORTCRUST PASTRY
8 oz (225 g) white flour
1 dessertspoon superfine sugar
6 oz (175 g) butter
2–3 tbsp water
1 egg yolk

FOR THE PIE
Shortcrust pastry
1 heaped tsp white flour
2 oz (60 g) superfine sugar
12 oz (350 g) blueberries
1 tbsp water
1 beaten egg white or milk for glaze (optional)
Serves 6–8

1 To make the pastry, mix together the flour and sugar, then rub in the butter bit by bit until the mixture resembles breadcrumbs. Beat 1 tbsp of water into the egg and add this to the flour. Work the mixture into a stiff dough, adding as much of the additional water as necessary. Chill in the refrigerator for at least 30 minutes before rolling out. (Thaw frozen ready-made pastry completely before using.)

2 Preheat the oven to 410°F (210°C, Gas Mark 7). Roll out half of the pastry and use to cover the bottom of an 7 or 8 in (18 cm) pie dish.

3 Mix the flour and superfine sugar and dust this all over the blueberries. Pile the fruit onto the pie base and add the water.

4 Roll out the remaining pastry into a round large enough to cover the fruit. Moisten the edges of the pastry and press them together. Make a hole in the top to allow steam to escape. Glaze with beaten egg white or milk.

5 Bake for 30–40 minutes. Cover the pastry loosely with foil to prevent overbrowning if necessary.

Damson jam

INGREDIENTS

For every 1 lb (450 g) of fruit allow (12 oz) (350g) granulated sugar

Peaches

1 Don't attempt to pit the damsons; it isn't worth the effort. Place all the fruit and half the sugar in layers in an earthenware bowl and leave to stand overnight or longer.

2 Place the fruit in a preserving pan, bring it slowly to the boil and simmer gently until the damsons are tender and start to disintegrate.

3 Add the remainder of the sugar and boil rapidly for 20–30 minutes until setting point is reached (see below).

4 Remove from the heat, skim off the pits and pour into preheated jam jars. Cool before putting on the lids.

Setting point Test for setting point when the jam has been boiling for 10–15 minutes. Put a little jam on a cold plate, cool it quickly and push the jam with your finger. If a definite crinkle forms, the jam is ready.

Container Kitchen Garden Calendar

VEGETABLE	WINTER			SPRING	
	EARLY	MID	LATE	EARLY	MID
Artichokes, Jerusalem	harvest			plant	
Beans, snap				sow	sow, plant out
bush					sow in cloches
pole					sow under glass
Beets					sow
Broccoli				sow	sow
Brussels sprouts	harvest				sow
Cabbage, fall & winter	harvest				sow
Chinese cabbage	harvest				sow
Carrots	harvest		sow early vars	sow	sow
Cauliflower, summer & fall				sow under glass	sow under glass
Celeriac				sow under glass	
Chard, Swiss & ruby	harvest				sow
Chicory	harvest forced				
Cress				sow	sow
Eggplants				sow under glass	prick out
Endive	harvest	harvest		sow curly	sow curly
Fennel, Florence					sow
Kale	harvest				sow
Kohlrabi					sow
Lettuce			sow	sow	sow
Onions			plant	plant	plant
Spring onions				sow	sow
Peas				sow	sow
Peppers				sow under glass	
Hot peppers				sow under glass	
Potatoes				sow	sow
Maincrop potatoes					sow
Pumpkins				sow under glass	
Radish			sow in cloches	sow	sow
Spinach	harvest			sow	sow, harvest
Perpetual beet	harvest			sow	harvest, sow
Summer Squash & Zucchini					sow under glass
Tomatoes, outdoor				sow under glass	sow under glass

LATE	SUMMER Early	Mid	Late	FALL Early	Mid	Late
					harvest, cover	harvest
sow	harvest	harvest	harvest	harvest		sow
sow	sow	harvest	harvest	harvest		
sow, plant out	sow		harvest	harvest	harvest	
sow	sow	harvest	harvest	harvest		
sow, plant out	plant out	plant out, harvest	harvest	harvest	harvest	
plant out					harvest	harvest
sow	plant out	plant out, harvest	harvest	harvest	harvest	harvest
sow	sow	sow	harvest	cover	cover	harvest
sow	sow, harvest	harvest	harvest	harvest	harvest	
plant out, sow		plant out	harvest	harvest	harvest	harvest
prick out	plant out				harvest	harvest
harvest, sow	sow, harvest	sow, harvest	harvest	harvest	harvest	harvest
sow forced vars	sow non-forced				harvest	harvest
sow	harvest	harvest, sow	harvest	harvest		
plant out	plant out		harvest	harvest		
sow Belgian	sow Belgian	sow curly	sow	cover, harvest	harvest	bring in to force
sow		harvest	harvest	harvest		
sow	plant out	plant out		harvest	harvest	harvest
sow	sow	sow	harvest	harvest	harvest	harvest
sow, harvest	harvest	harvest	harvest	harvest		
			harvest, store	harvest, store		
sow	harvest	harvest	harvest	harvest		
sow	harvest	harvest				
	plant out		harvest	harvest		
	plant out		harvest	harvest		
		harvest	harvest			
				harvest	harvest	
	plant out		harvest	harvest		
sow, harvest	sow, harvest	harvest	harvest	harvest		
sow	harvest	harvest	harvest, sow	harvest, sow	harvest	harvest
harvest, sow	harvest		harvest	harvest	harvest	harvest
sow under glass	plant out, sow		harvest	harvest		
plant out	plant out		harvest	harvest		

Herb Properties

HERB	CULINARY	MEDICINAL	SCENTED	FLOWERING
Achillea millefolium (Yarrow)	●	●		●
Adonis vernalis (Spring Adonis)		●		●
Agastache foeniculum (Anise Hyssop)	●	●	●	●
Allium schoenoprasum (Chives)	●			●
Aloysia triphylla (Lemon Verbena)	●	●	●	
Anethum graveolens (Dill)	●			●
Anthriscus cerefolium (Chervil)	●			
Armeria maritima (Thrift)		●		●
Arnica montana (Arnica)		●		●
Artemisia dracunculus (French Tarragon)	●			
Artemisia vulgaris (Mugwort)		●		
Bellis perennis (Daisy)	●	●		●
Borago officinalis (Borage)	●	●		●
Calamintha grandiflora (Garden Calamint)		●	●	●
Calendula officinalis (English Marigold)	●	●		●
Cardamine pratensis (Lady's Smock)	●	●		●
Carum carvi (Caraway)	●			
Centaurea cyanus (Cornflower)		●		●
Chamaemelum nobile (Lawn Chamomile)		●	●	●
Coriandrum sativum (Coriander)	●	●		●
Daucus carota (Wild Carrot)		●		
Dianthus caryophyllus (Clove Pink)	●		●	●
Echinacea purpurea (Purple Coneflower)		●		●
Echium vulgare (Viper's Bugloss)	●	●		●
Eschscholzia californica (California Poppy)		●		●
Filipendula ulmaria (Meadowsweet)	●	●		●
Galium odoratum (Sweet Woodruff)		●	●	
Geranium robertianum (Herb Robert)		●		
Geum urbanum (Herb Bennet)	●	●		
Helichrysum italicum ssp. *serotinum* (Curry Plant)				
Heliotropium arborescens (Heliotrope)			●	●
Hesperis matronalis (Sweet Rocket)	●			
Humulus lupulus (Hop)	●	●		●
Hyssopus officinalis (Hyssop)	●	●	●	●

HERB	CULINARY	MEDICINAL	SCENTED	FLOWERING
Jasminum officinale (Jasmine)	●		●	●
Juniperus communis (Juniper)	●			
Laurus nobilis (Sweet Bay)	●			
Lavandula (Lavender)		●	●	●
Leucanthemum vulgare (Ox-eye Daisy)	●	●		●
Matricaria recutita (Wild Chamomile)	●		●	●
Melissa officinalis (Lemon Balm)	●		●	
Mentha x *piperata* (Peppermint)	●	●	●	●
Mentha pulegium (Pennyroyal)	●	●		
Meum athamanticum (Spignel)	●			●
Monarda didyma (Bergamot)	●		●	●
Myrrhis odorata (Sweet Cicely)	●	●		
Nigella sativa (Love-in-a-Mist)	●	●		●
Ocimum basilicum (Sweet Basil)	●			
Origanum majorana (Sweet Marjoram)	●			●
Origanum vulgare (Oregano)	●			
Pelargonium (Scented Geranium)	●		●	●
Perilla frutescens (Perilla)	●		●	
Petroselinum crispum (Parsley)	●	●		
Primula vulgaris (Primrose)	●	●	●	●
Pycnanthemum pilosum (Mountain Mint)	●		●	●
Rosa rugosa (Hedgehog Rose)	●		●	●
Rosmarinus officinalis (Rosemary)	●	●		
Salvia officinalis (Common Sage)	●	●		●
Sanguisorba minor syn. *Poterium sanguisorba* (Salad Burnet)	●			
Silybum marianum (Milk Thistle)	●	●		●
Smyrnium olusatrum (Black Lovage)	●	●	●	
Stachys officinalis (Betony)		●		
Tagetes patula (French Marigold)	●		●	●
Tanacetum parthenium (Feverfew)		●		●
Tanacetum vulgare (Tansy)	●	●		●
Thymus vulgaris (Thyme)	●			●
Tropaeolum majus (Nasturtium)	●	●		●
Viola odorata (Sweet Violet)	●	●	●	●

Plants for Sun and Shade

SUN

HERB

Achillea millefolium (Yarrow)

Allium sativum (Garlic)

Allium schoenoprasum (Chives)

Anethum graveolens (Dill)

Armeria maritima (Thrift)

Artemisia dracunculus
 (French Tarragon)

Artemesia vulgaris (Mugwort)

Borago officinalis (Borage)

Calendula officinalis
 (English Marigold)

Carum carvi (Caraway)

Centaurea cyanus (Cornflower)

Centaurea scabiosa (Greater Knapweed)

Chamaemelum nobile
 (Lawn Chamomile)

Coriandrum sativum (Coriander)

Daucus carota (Wild Carrot)

Dianthus caryophyllus (Clove Pink)

Echium vulgare (Viper's Bugloss)

Eschscholzia californica
 (California Poppy)

Heliotropium arborescens (Heliotrope)

Humulus lupulus (Hop)

Hyssopus officinalis (Hyssop)

Lavandula (Lavender)

Leucanthemum vulgare
 (Ox-eye Daisy)

Mentha x piperata (Peppermint)

Nigella sativa (Love-in-a-Mist)

Ocimum basilicum (Sweet Basil)

Origanum majorana (Sweet Marjoram)

Pelargonium (Scented Geranium)

Portaluca oleracea (Wild Purslane)

Pycnanthemum pilosum
 (Mountain Mint)

Salvia officinalis (Common Sage)

Sanguisorba minor syn. *Poterium sanguisorba* (Salad Burnet)

Satureja hortensis (Summer Savory)

Silybum marianum (Milk Thistle)

Smyrnium olusatrum (Black Lovage)

Tagetes patula (French Marigold)

Tanacetum parthenium (Feverfew)

Tanacetum vulgare (Tansy)

Thymus vulgaris (Thyme)

Tropaeolum majus (Nasturtium)

Viola tricolor (Heartsease)

VEGETABLE

Beans, Green (*Phaseolus vulgaris*)
 Runner (*Phaseolus coccineus*)

Broccoli (*Brassica oleracea*
 Italica Group)

Cabbage (*Brassica oleracea*
 Capitata Group)

Carrot (*Daucus carota*)

Chicory (*Cichorium intybus*)

Chinese cabbage
 (*Brassica rapa* Pekinensis Group)

Cucumber (*Cucumis sativus*)

Eggplant (*Solanum melongena*)

Endive (*Cichorium endiva*)

Florence fennel (*Foeniculum vulgare*
 Azoricum Group)

Mustard (*Sinapsis alba*)

Onion (*Allium cepa* Aggregatum

Group)

Peppers, sweet
 (*Capsicum annuum* Grassum Group)

Potatoes (*Solanum tuberosum*)

Pumpkin (*Cucurbita maxima*)

Summer squash, Zucchini (*Cucurbita
 pepo*)

Tomato (*Lycopersicon esculentum*)

FRUIT

Apples (*Malus domestica*)

Apricots (*Prunus armeniaca*)

Blackcurrants (*Ribes nigrum*)

Blackberries & hybrids (*Rubus
 fruticosus*)

Cherries, sweet (*Prunus avium*)

Citrus fruit (*Citrus sinensis, C. limon*)

Figs (*Ficus carica*)

Medlars (*Mespilus germanica*)

Nectarines (*Prunus persica*
 var. *nectarina*)

Olive (*Olea europaea*)

Peaches (*Prunus persica*)

Pears (*Pyrus communis*)

Plums, gages & damsons
 (*Prunus domestica, P. institia*)

Quinces (*Cydonia oblonga*)

Strawberries (*Fragaria x ananassa*)

PARTIAL SHADE

HERB

Achillea millefolium (Yarrow)

Adonis vernalis (Spring Adonis)

Anthriscus cerefolium (Chervil)

Arctostaphylos uva-ursi (Bearberry)

Bellis perennis (Daisy)

Calamintha grandiflora
   (Garden Calamint)

Chamaemelum nobile
   (Lawn Chamomile)

Crocus sativus (Saffron Crocus)

Filipendula ulmaria (Meadowsweet)

Galium odoratum (Sweet Woodruff)

Geranium robertianum (Herb Robert)

Geum urbanum (Herb Bennet)

Hesperis matronalis (Sweet Rocket)

Juniperus communis (Juniper)

Laurus nobilis (Sweet Bay)

Melissa officinalis (Lemon Balm)

Mentha pulegium (Mint)

Mentha spicata (Spearmint)

Meum athamanticum (Spignel)

Monarda didyma (Bergamot)

Myrrhis odorata (Sweet Cicely)

Origanum majorana (Sweet Marjoram)

Origanum vulgare (Oregano)

Perilla frutescens (Perilla)

Primula veris (Cowslip)

Primula vulgaris (Primrose)

Rosa rugosa (Rose)

Tanacetum parthenium (Feverfew)

Tanacetum vulgare (Tansy)

Viola odorata (Sweet Violet)

VEGETABLE

Artichoke, Jerusalem
   (*Helianthus tuberosus*)

Beet (*Beta vulgaris*)

Beet, Perpetual (*Beta vulgaris*
   Cicla Group)

Cabbage (*Brassica oleracea*
   Capitata Group)

Chard, ruby (*Beta vulgaris* Cicla Group)

Kale (*Brassica oleracea*
   Acephala Group)

Land Cress (*Lepidium sativum*)

Lettuce (*Lactuca sativa*)

Pea (*Pisum sativum*)

Radish (*Raphanus sativus*)

   Turnip (*Brassica campestris*
   Rapifera Group)

FRUIT

Apples (*Malus domestica*)

Blackcurrants (*Ribes nigrum*)

Blackberries & hybrids (*Rubus*
   fruticosus)

Blueberries (*Vaccinium corymbosum*)

Cherries, sweet (*Prunus avium*)

Gooseberries (*Ribes uva-crispa*)

Medlars (*Mespilus germanica*)

Red & whitecurrants (*Ribes rubrum*)

Plums, gages & damsons
   (*Prunus domestica, P. institia*)

Wild Strawberry (*Fragaria vesca*)

SHADE

HERB

Achillea millefolium (Yarrow)

Anthriscus cerefolium (Chervil)

Arctostaphylos uva-ursi (Bearberry)

Calamintha grandiflora
   (Garden Calamint)

Cardamine pratensis (Lady's Smock)

Galium odoratum (Sweet Woodruff)

Geranium robertianum (Herb Robert)

Myrrhis odorata (Sweet Cicely)

Origanum vulgare (Oregano)

Perilla frutescens (Perilla)

Primula vulgaris (Primrose)

Rosa spp. (Rose) A number are suitable
for growing on north walls

Stachys officinalis (Betony)

Viola odorata (Sweet Violet)

VEGETABLE

Artichoke, Jerusalem
   (*Helianthus tuberosus*)

Chard, ruby (*Beta vulgaris* Cicla Group)

Kale (*Brassica oleracea*
   Acephala Group)

Land Cress (*Lepidium sativum*)

Lettuce (*Lactuca sativa*)

Spinach (*Spinacea oleracea*)

FRUIT

Blackcurrants (*Ribes nigrum*)

Cherries, acid (*Prunus avium*)

Gooseberries (*Ribes uva-crispa*)

Wild Strawberry (*Fragaria vesca*)

NOTE: Apart from Morello cherries,
fruit will not flourish in complete shade.

Zone Map

The zone map gives an indication of the average winter temperatures that can be expected in a given geographical location. Plants vary in their requirements. Use the zones as a guide.

Plant hardiness zones are determined by the average number of frost-free days each year and the lowest winter temperatures. In botanical terms they indicate the lowest temperatures at which a plant is likely to survive. At the other end of the scale the majority of herbs and fruit will tolerate temperatures up to 90°F (32°C).

Vegetables and annual plants are not given a zone for they complete their growing cycle in one year, however a number of vegetables will not tolerate extremely high temperatures. It must be remembered that all zones and temperature indications are only a guide. Each site is different and each one will contain a number of micro-climates created by sheltered walls, hedges or trees, while windowsills may be exposed, open to the wind and rain; a patio may well be an unexpected frost pocket.

You need to experiment to discover what will grow in various containers. Many plants are adaptable and will grow in sun and shade and if a plant will not flourish in the conditions you can offer it, abandon it and find another that will.

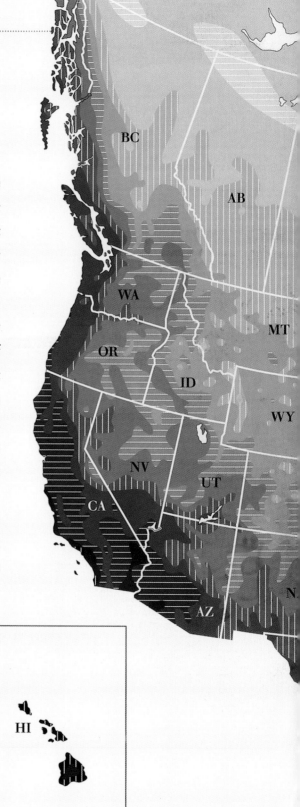

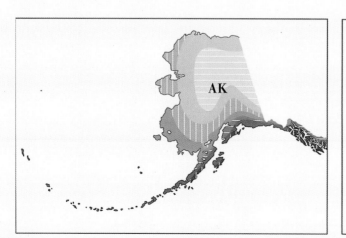

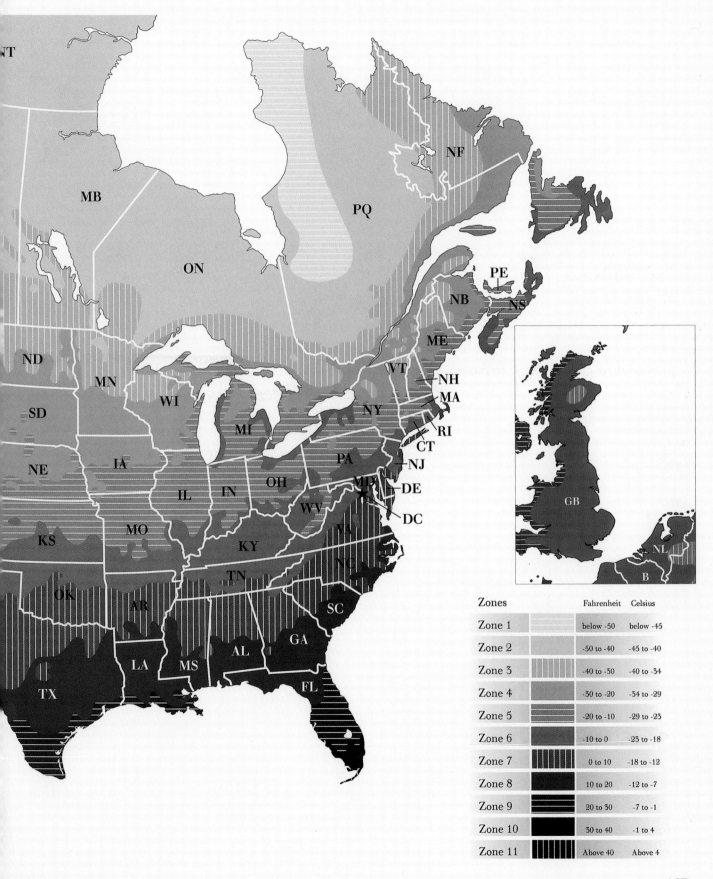

Zones		Fahrenheit	Celsius
Zone 1		below -50	below -45
Zone 2		-50 to -40	-45 to -40
Zone 3		-40 to -30	-40 to -34
Zone 4		-30 to -20	-34 to -29
Zone 5		-20 to -10	-29 to -23
Zone 6		-10 to 0	-23 to -18
Zone 7		0 to 10	-18 to -12
Zone 8		10 to 20	-12 to -7
Zone 9		20 to 30	-7 to -1
Zone 10		30 to 40	-1 to 4
Zone 11		Above 40	Above 4

Index

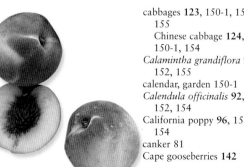

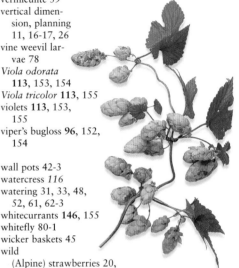

Acknowledgments

Picture credits:
(Key: R–Right, L–Left, T–Top, M–Middle, C–Centre, B–Bottom)
p.2 (BR) Clive Nichols/Sir Terence Conran; p4/5 Graham Strong/Clive Nichols; p6/7 Clive Nichols/Barnsley House. Glos; P7 (TR) Andrew Lawson; p8/9 Clive Nichols/Jane Nichols; p10 (TL) Clive Nichols/Jane Hogben; p11 Graham Strong/Clive Nichols; p12 (BL) Clive Nichols/Jane Nichols; (TL) Marie O'Hara/G.P.L.; p14 (BL) Clive Nichols/Designer: Jane Nichols; (TL) Andrew Lawson; p17 (TR) Andrew Lawson; p20 (TL) John Glover/G.P.L.; p21 Steven Wooster/ The Old Rectory, Sudborough; p22 (BL) Andrew Lawson; p23 (TR) Clive Nichols/Jane Nichols; p24 (B) Clive Nichols/Sir Terence Conran; p26 (BL) Clive Nichols/Jane Nichols; p27 Clive Nichols/Sir Terence Conran; p28 (B) Andrew Lawson; p29 Steven Wooster; p30 London Roof Garden designed by Dan Pearson/Steven Wooster; p31 Andrew Lawson; p34 (BL) Andrew Lawson/ Powys Castle, Powys; p35 Steven Wooster; p36 (BL) Andrew Lawson; p38/39 Clive Nichols/Barnsley House, Glos; p47 Ron Sutherland/G.P.L.; p54 (BL) Steven Wooster; p55 Lynne Brotchie/G.P.L.; p78 (L to R) Garden and Wildlife Matter Photo Library; Howard Rice/G.P.L.; Howard Rice/G.P.L.; Vaughan Fleming/G.P.L.; p79 (L to R) Sheila Apps/Wildlife Matters; Howard Rice/G.P.L.; Colin Milkins/Garden Matters Colin Milkins/Garden Matters Michael Howes/G.P.L.; p80 (L to R) Michael Howes/G.P.L.; Holt Studios International; John Phipps/Garden Matters; p81 (TL) Howard Rice/G.P.L.; (BL to BR) John Glover/G.P.L.; Howard Rice/G.P.L.; Garden and Wildlife Matters; Lamontagne/G.P.L.; p84/85 Clive Nichols/Jane Nichols; p111 Jerry Pavia/G.P.L.; p112 Howard Rice; p113 Howard Rice; p115 Mayer/Le Scanff/G.P.L.; p116 Mayer/Le Scanff/G.P.L.; p128 Steven Wooster; p145 Wildlife Matters.
All other photographs are copyright Collins & Brown.